JOSS NAYLOR'S
LAKES, MERES AND WATERS OF
THE LAKE DISTRICT

Loweswater to Over Water: 105 miles in the footsteps of a legend

By Vivienne Crow with Joss Naylor

Photography by Stephen Wilson

© Vivienne Crow with Joss Naylor 2021
First edition 2021
ISBN: 978 1 78631 087 3

Printed in Singapore by KHL Printing.

A catalogue record for this book is available from the British Library.

Route mapping by Lovell Johns
www.lovelljohns.com
© Crown copyright 2021 OS PU100012932.
NASA relief data courtesy of ESRI

Cicerone
Juniper House, Murley Moss,
Oxenholme Road, Kendal
Cumbria LA9 7RL
www.cicerone.co.uk

Photography by Stephen Wilson (www.granddayoutphotography.co.uk) unless otherwise stated.

Every effort has been made to trace and contact copyright holders of archive photos reproduced in this book. Any errors or omissions will be rectified in future reprints of the book if drawn to our attention.

This book was written, researched and photography taken during the COVID-19 pandemic. Social-distancing rules at the time were adhered to.

With thanks to the Fell Runners Association and the Achille Ratti Climbing Club for permission to reproduce content.

Front cover: Wasdale sunset from the slopes of Yewbarrow, showing the farmhouse at Bowderdale (right) and with Joss Naylor inset

Pages 2–3: Ennerdale Water in autumn (Chapter 2)

Right: The road snakes its way along the shores of Wastwater (Chapter 2)

ADVICE TO READERS

While every effort is made by our authors to ensure the accuracy of our books as they go to print, changes can occur during the lifetime of an edition. Any updates that we know of for this book will be on the Cicerone website (www.cicerone.co.uk/1087/updates). We are always grateful for information about any discrepancies between a book and the facts on the ground, sent by email to updates@cicerone.co.uk or by post to Cicerone, Juniper House, Murley Moss, Oxenholme Road, Kendal, LA9 7RL.
Register your book: To sign up to receive free updates, special offers and GPX files where available, register your book at www.cicerone.co.uk.

CONTENTS

Map key 6
Overview map 7

ACKNOWLEDGEMENTS		9
FOREWORD		10
INTRODUCTION		13
Chapter 1	Loweswater to Ennerdale. 21
Chapter 2	Ennerdale to Eskdale Green 33
Chapter 3	Eskdale Green to Dunnerdale 44
Chapter 4	Dunnerdale to Coniston 59
Chapter 5	Coniston to Skelwith Bridge 71
Chapter 6	Skelwith Bridge to Troutbeck 83
Chapter 7	Troutbeck to Haweswater 95
Chapter 8	Haweswater to Glenridding 109
Chapter 9	Glenridding to Keswick 121
Chapter 10	Keswick to Over Water 132
Appendix A	Marshals and split times for Joss's 1983 LMW	148
Appendix B	The 27 lakes, meres and waters	149
Appendix C	Glossary of dialect terms and topographical features	150
Appendix D	Route summary table	150
Appendix E	Some of Joss's challenge runs	151

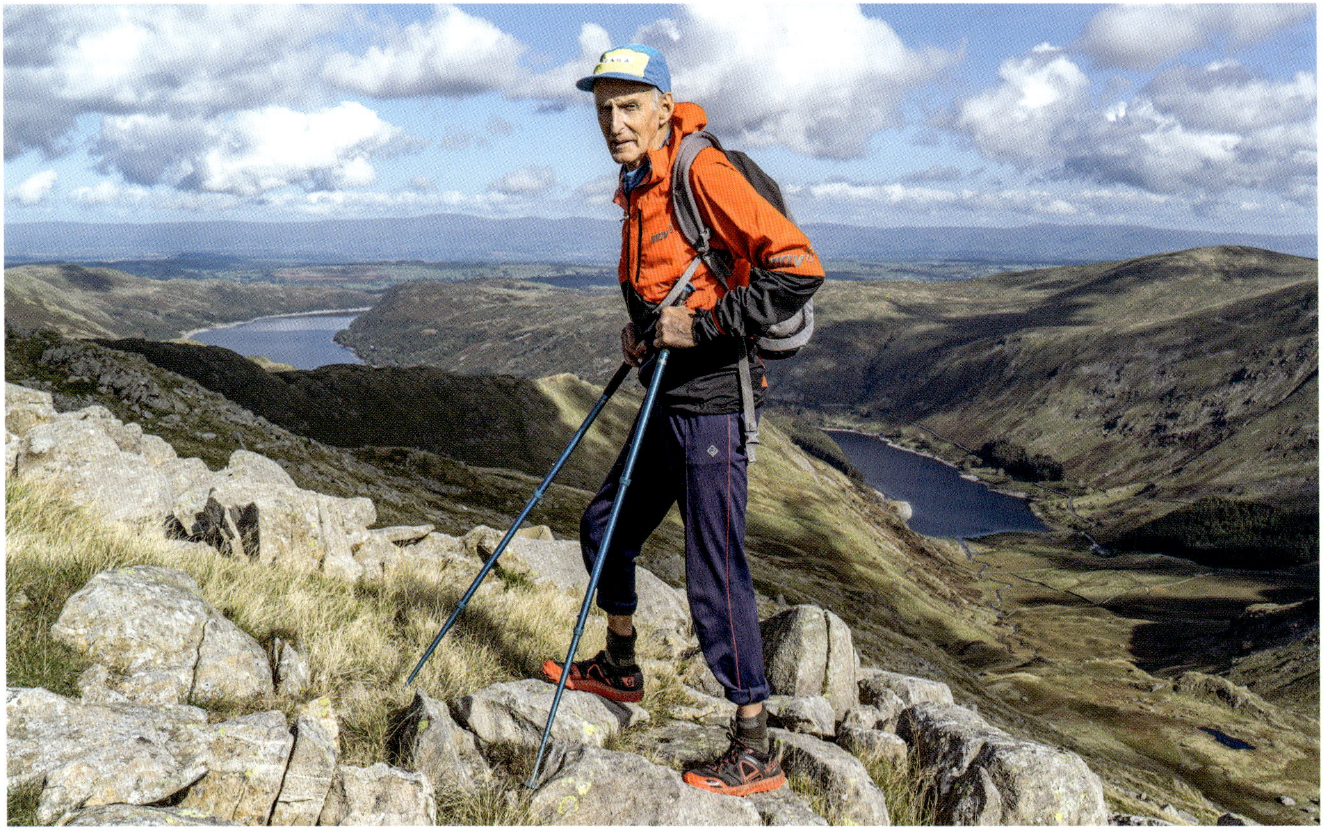

▲ On the fells above Haweswater, with the North Pennines visible in the distance (Chapter 8)

SYMBOLS USED ON MAPS

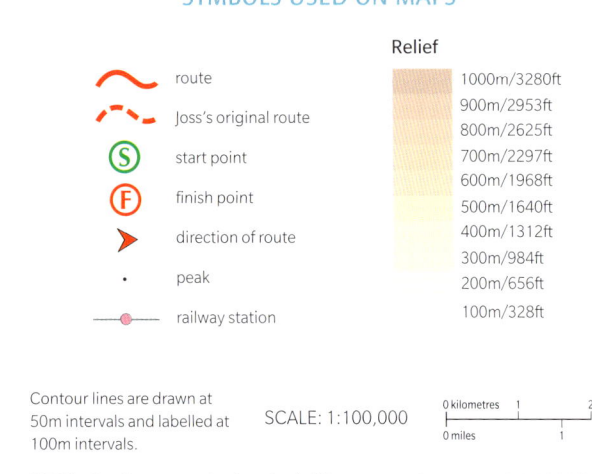

Contour lines are drawn at 50m intervals and labelled at 100m intervals.

SCALE: 1:100,000

GPX files for all routes can be downloaded free at www.cicerone.co.uk/1087/GPX.

MOUNTAIN SAFETY

Any walk or run that takes in fells or mountains has its dangers, and the route described in this book is no exception. All who venture into the mountains should recognise this and take responsibility for themselves and their companions along the way. The authors and publisher have made every effort to ensure that the information contained in this book was correct when it went to press, but, except for any liability that cannot be excluded by law, they cannot accept responsibility for any loss, injury or inconvenience sustained by any person using this book.

In the UK, to call out the Mountain Rescue, **ring 999**: this will connect you via any available network. Once connected to the emergency operator, ask for the police.

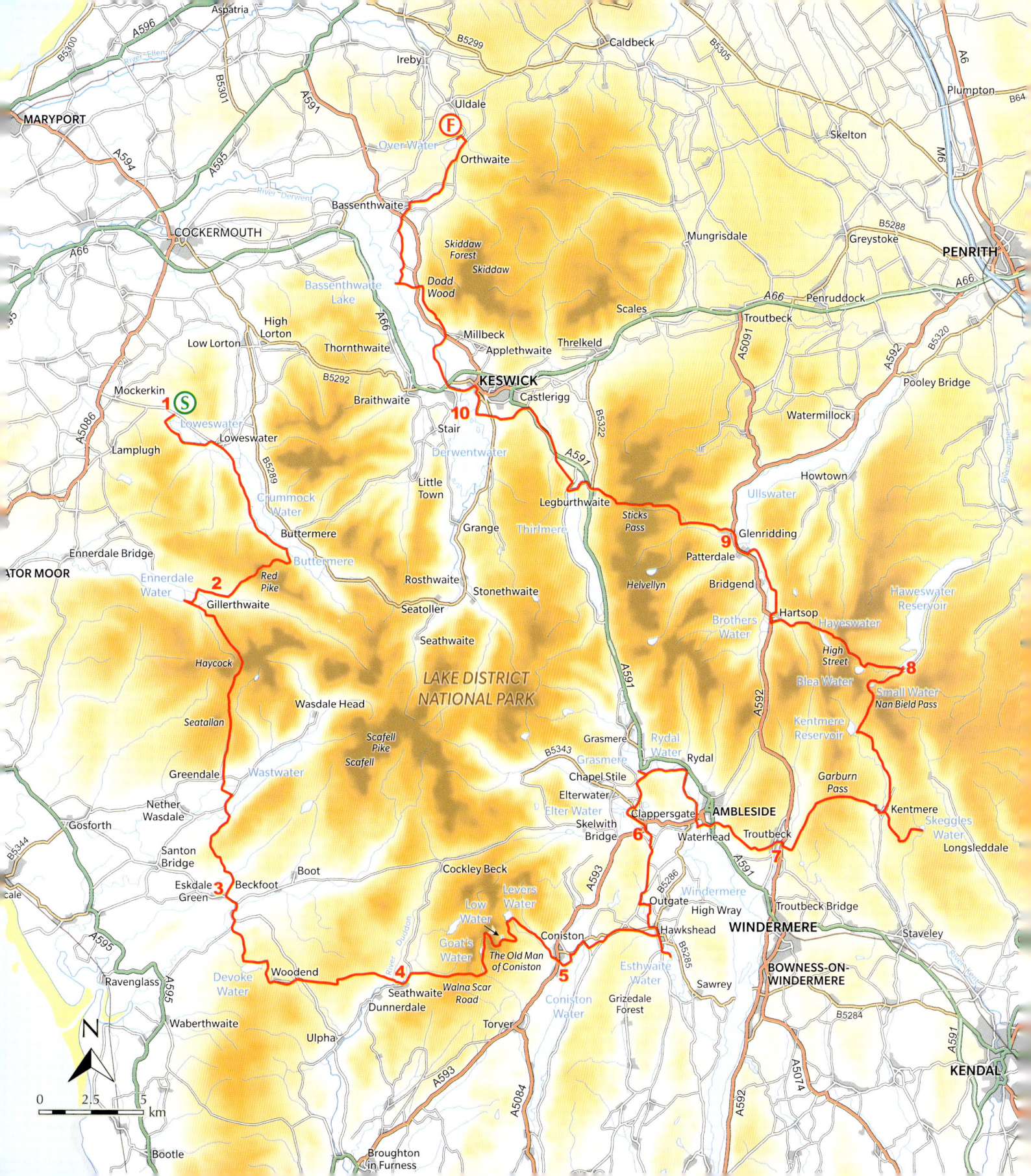

ACKNOWLEDGEMENTS

A large number of people went out of their way to make this book possible, doing everything from helping track down Joss's running companions to sharing their cherished memories of a very special day on the fells. My apologies to anyone who feels they have been missed off the following list; it's nothing personal, but some of the details have been lost, or at best blurred, by the passage of time.

I would like to thank, in no particular order, Ken Ledward, Charmian Heaton of the Fell Runners Association (FRA), writer Steve Chilton, Rob Allen, Rob Green of the Achille Ratti Climbing Club, Ryan Todhunter, Carl Bell, Chris Chinn, Ben Chinn, Ian Finlay, Jean Nelson, Dave Woodhead, David Weatherhead, Des Gibbons, Paul Tierney, Sarah McCormack and Steve Watts.

The following runners and marshals provided memories, photos and words of encouragement: John Wild, Alastair Young, Iain Irving, Alex Smith, Richard Eastman, Phil Atherton, Nigel Alderson, Tom Bell and Andrew Simpson. Other archive photography was provided by John Cleare and Tommy Orr.

Excerpts from the late Leo Pollard's account of his 1981 route are reproduced with the kind permission of the Achille Ratti Climbing Club. Back copies of the FRA's *The Fell Runner* magazine were invaluable, particularly for research into Joss's lifetime of achievements and for Alex Smith's write-up of the day.

I'd like to extend a special thank you to David Frazer, for introducing me to Joss, and to the members of 'Team Joss' for turning the summer of 2020 into 'summat special' – they are Stephen Wilson, Dave Elliott, Pete Todhunter and, of course, Joss himself. The quality of Stephen's superb photography, used throughout this book, speaks for itself. Dave's memories and photographs of the 1983 run as well as his help with tracking down marshals and runners were crucial to the background work. Pete was instrumental in getting this project off the ground, organising our days on the fells, tracking down archive images, carrying out detailed research, tirelessly answering every question I threw at him and, let's not forget, holding gates open. And Joss was just Joss – an absolute legend.

Vivienne Crow
July 2021

▲ The 2020 team – from left, Stephen Wilson, Dave Elliott, Joss, Pete Todhunter and Vivienne Crow (Photo credit: Vivienne Crow)

◀ Elter Water with the Langdale Pikes in the distance (Chapter 6)

FOREWORD

Back in June 1983, I ran all 27 of the lakes, meres and waters. It gave me an opportunity to have a good look at the Lake District and to visit places where I wouldn't normally have gone. I've covered a tremendous amount of ground in the National Park over the years, but this was one of the most picturesque things I ever did. It was a lovely, sunny day, and it made me realise that I lived in the most beautiful part of the world. The Lake District has everything, and I feel very honoured to have called it my home for the last 85 years. It was a magic day, and I hope that the people who buy this book get as much pleasure out of reading it and looking at the pictures as I got from running the route.

I would like to thank everyone who made that day possible – all the marshals, runners and the support team – because it's one that has always stuck in my memory. I hope too that they enjoyed it as much as I did, because it was something very, very special.

My part of the proceeds from sales of this book will go to the Brathay Trust, a local charity that mostly helps young people from deprived areas. It really does turn their lives around and I'm proud to support it. I am delighted that Cicerone as publishers will be matching my share – effectively doubling the contribution to Brathay.

Joss Naylor MBE
July 2021

Joss Naylor and Lassie on the Lake District fells ▶

INTRODUCTION

A round of the National Park's lakes, meres and waters

'It's summat special, like.' Ask Lake District fell-running legend Joss Naylor why he always describes the Lakes, Meres and Waters (LMW) as one of the best routes he ever ran, and that is the answer you'll invariably receive. Spend an entire summer with him – rewalking the route, chatting about his memories of it, immersing yourself in it – and you begin to understand that it was one of those moments in his life when landscape and weather, and mind and body, were perfectly aligned. On that day in June 1983, when Joss was 47 years old, everything just came together – and he was able to visit 27 of the Lake District's largest bodies of water, running 105 miles over fells and along valleys, in little more than 19 hours, a record that still stands.

'It's summat you couldn't really explain to anybody,' he says when pressed further. 'It was like a dream. It was, honestly! My legs just went well all day, I never had a bad patch. I ran all the hills at a steady pace – I was legging on to be honest – and it wasn't draining me body. It was just good, relaxed running, over all sorts of terrain, and it continued like that all day.

'Looking back afterwards, I thought how privileged I was to have done it because it's a beautiful thing to do. It gave us a chance to have a good look at the Lake District and go to places where you don't usually go. I don't know why more people don't do it. The likes of the Bob Graham and that are flogged to death, but you see the valley bottoms more on this – you get a better view. It's one of the most picturesque things anyone can do. The Lake District is one of the nicest places in the world.'

The route was the brainchild of fell-runner Dave Meek, but the first person to complete it was Leo Pollard in 1981. Dave originally envisaged a round of the National Park's lakes, meres and waters, starting and finishing in the same place, but it was Leo who got a map out and realised that Dave's list missed out two of the bodies of water named on the Ordnance Survey sheet – Skeggles Water and Over Water. With their inclusion, the chance of ever completing the challenge as a round and within 24 hours became almost impossible. Leo made an attempt at a round with Pete Schofield in 1980, but it was abandoned. 'I soon realised that to keep the Lakeland 24-hour tradition alive the route had to be a point to point,' Leo

◀ Ennerdale Water (Chapter 2)

▲ *Clockwise from top left:* Joss Naylor touches Loweswater at the start of his 1983 run (Stage 1) (Photo credit: Dave Elliott); with Pete Trainor on the Pennine Way in 1974 (Photo credit: Tommy Orr); Joss in 1971 at Dunmail Raise during his first 24-Hour Fell Record, with Alan Walker (left) and Fred Rogerson (Photo from Joss's own collection; photographer unknown); tackling the Welsh Three Thousanders in 1973 (Photo credit: © John Cleare/mountaincamera)

later wrote in an account of the run for the Achille Ratti Climbing Club. 'To give the best advantage, Loweswater to Over Water or Over Water to Loweswater.' This route, he felt, also benefitted from keeping 'the percentage of road to fell down'. With members of the climbing club supporting him and accompanying him as pacemakers, he completed what became known as the '26 Lake, Meres and Waters' [sic] in 35hr 29min in 'atrocious' conditions in June 1981. The following year, Alan Heaton managed it in 25hr 16min.

When Joss heard about the route, he already had several major fell-running achievements under his belt and held a number of important records. He'd broken the 24-Hour Fell Record on three separate occasions in the early 1970s, clocking up 61 peaks in June 1971 (before that, Alan Heaton had managed 60 in July 1965), 63 peaks in June 1972 and then extending that to a massive 72 peaks during a heatwave in June 1975. It was a record that had seemed unassailable – until 13 years later, in June 1988, when Mark McDermott added another four peaks to the total. (At the time of writing, the men's record-holder was Kim Collison, who managed 78 peaks in July 2020, while the women's record of 65 peaks was taken by Carol Morgan in August 2020.)

In July 1971, less than two weeks after his first 24-Hour Fell Record, Joss completed the fastest National Three Peaks Challenge, climbing Snowdon, Scafell Pike and Ben Nevis in 11hr 54min – achieved with the help of rally driver and climbing shop owner Frank Davies at the wheel of a souped-up Ford Capri. He'd also run the Welsh 1000m Peaks in 3hr 37min (1972), broken the record for the 14 Welsh Three Thousanders (4hr 46min in 1973), taken the record for the Pennine Way (3 days 4hr 35min in 1974) and won countless fell races and Mountain Trials. (His historic seven-day round of the Wainwrights, a record that stood for 28 years, would follow in 1986.)

Joss was good friends with Leo, and when he heard about Leo's massive Lakeland odyssey, he thought it 'sounded like a nice thing to do' – and, of course, he might manage to topple yet another fell-running record in the process. Joss being Joss though – very much his own man – he decided to add Kentmere Reservoir to the existing list of 26 bodies of water. It meant dropping into Kentmere, climbing out (to visit Skeggles Water) and then dropping back into the valley again, but he wasn't put off. Fitting it in between work on his farm at Bowderdale, Wasdale, and his job as a storeman at the Sellafield nuclear reprocessing site, he managed a recce of the entire route the weekend before he was due to attempt the run.

Beginning at Loweswater, the route visits Crummock Water and Buttermere then goes over the high fells into Ennerdale, along Wasdale and Eskdale, over into Dunnerdale, across pathless ground on the Coniston Fells, down to Coniston Water and through the valleys to Windermere, into Kentmere, up and over the Nan Bield Pass to Haweswater, back over the fells and down to Ullswater, over Sticks Pass to Thirlmere and then on to Derwentwater and Bassenthwaite Lake before ending at Over Water. Joss calculated he could do it in 19hr 20min, which would have shaved nearly six hours off Alan Heaton's time. The night before the big day, he informed Fred Rogerson, who maintained records for this and other fell-running challenges, of his intentions. Despite Joss's reputation, Fred was sceptical. Joss recalls: 'He asked me, "What time you coming through?" I told him and he said, "There's some bloody chance of that".' The rest, as they say, is history...

Thirty-five years later, with Joss now in his 80s, he decided he wanted to create a permanent record of that amazing day – a day that is as much a part of fell-running folklore as it is a part of one man's personal story. He also wanted to share the route with others – walkers and runners alike – so they could follow in his footsteps. With the help of his friend and fellow fell-runner Pete Todhunter, he began to build a team to make this possible. The result was that, in the summer of 2020, I joined Joss, Pete, Dave Elliott (a crucial part of the support team in 1983) and photographer Stephen Wilson in the Lake District, rewalking much of the LMW.

As everyone will recall, it was a summer like no other. The COVID-19 pandemic meant our original plans had to be shelved and new strategies developed as the situation evolved. We'd wanted to get out walking as soon as Joss returned from his annual winter sojourn in Spain, but lockdown put paid to that. We'd also planned to walk linear sections of the route, leaping in and out of each other's cars as we moved around the National Park, but social-distancing rules and the risk of infection made that unthinkable. Okay, so Joss may be one of the fittest, healthiest 84-year-olds anyone could ever hope to meet, but we had to bear in mind that he was in a vulnerable age group. He'd also had a bout of pneumonia the previous year, so we kept a watchful eye on the infection rates throughout Cumbria, ready to cancel planned walks should the figures begin to rise. Like everyone else, we had to adjust to a new, constantly changing reality.

Joss didn't want to delay it; he'd been toying with the idea of turning his legendary run into a book for several years now and he wasn't getting any younger. He also wanted to create something that would feed into the fundraising efforts of his favourite charity, the Brathay Trust, for years to come. The Ambleside-based organisation works to improve the life chances of children and young people, particularly those from deprived backgrounds, through engagement in challenging outdoor and creative activities. 'It does a tremendous

> He decided to add Kentmere Reservoir to the existing list

▲ Joss on Middle Fell, with the mountains of Wasdale Head behind him (Chapter 2)

Introduction 17

▲ Joss on the fells above Kentmere (Chapter 7)

> 'These kids come to Brathay and the Lake District and they're inspired. It can really turn their lives around'

job,' says Joss, who is patron of the charity's 10in10 marathon challenge. 'When you see the upbringing some of these kids have...it's probably one of the most worthy charities in the country.

'When I first moved to Bowderdale, this chappie, a schoolmaster from Moss Side in Manchester, used to bring a bunch of kids on holiday. A lot of them had never seen grass before, let alone a cow. I was milking one morning, and two or three came in to buy some, and as they opened their mouths, I squirted milk in. They thought it was bloody magic. They'd thought it just come out of a bottle. Kids like those ones, they come to Brathay and the Lake District, and they're inspired by what they see and do. They go home from there and they see the world in a different light. It really can turn their lives around.'

So, on 24 June 2020 – coincidentally just one day short of the 37th anniversary of Joss's LMW record-breaker – the various members of 'Team Joss' met at Loweswater to begin the journey to Over Water. Although it took a little longer than 19hr 14min, we managed to rewalk almost all of the route that summer. And do you know what? Joss is right; it really is 'summat special'.

▲ Joss beside Wastwater, his 'home lake' (Chapter 2)

A CONFUSING NOTE ON NAMING

The Achille Ratti Climbing Club coordinates the fell-running challenge known as the '26 Lake, Meres and Waters', which visits all the bodies of water named as 'lakes', 'meres' or 'waters' on the 1958 one-inch Ordnance Survey map of the Lake District.

Now, the observant will have noted that the name of the challenge features the word 'lake' rather than 'lakes'. That's because there is only one 'lake' in the 'Lake' District with the word 'lake' in its name – Bassenthwaite Lake. That doesn't mean, though, that there is only one 'lake' in the 'Lake' District. (Don't let anyone tell you otherwise!) Many of the 'meres' and the 'waters' are technically valley-bottom, ribbon lakes. They're interchangeable terms. (Don't let anyone tell you there's a lake called 'Lake Windermere' either. There isn't, because that would be tautological, wouldn't it? You're getting the hang of this now, aren't you?) A few of the 'meres' and 'waters' are reservoirs too, although even these usually started life as smaller ribbon lakes – or as 'tarns'. Ah yes! Tarns…

Just to confuse matters, several of the 'waters' listed on the 1958 one-inch Ordnance Survey map are indeed 'tarns'. Strictly speaking, tarns are mountain pools, sometimes formed in corries as a result of glacial action. I say 'strictly speaking' because there are a few tarns in lowland areas too. Generally though, if it's in a valley, it's a ribbon lake; if it's on the fells, it's a tarn. I'm glad we cleared that up.

ABOUT THIS BOOK

Joss hopes this book will inspire walkers and runners to follow in his footsteps – or provide armchair travellers and would-be wanderers with a fresh perspective on his beloved Lake District.

His 1983 journey has been broken down into 10 sections, each of which can be walked in a day. These range in length from 9 miles (14.5km) to 13.9 miles (22.4km). Notes at the end of each chapter provide a guide to the recommended route, which sticks as close to Joss's original run as possible. In a few places, alternative routes have been suggested – to keep to established paths, for example, or where there is no public access.

Readers should be aware though that these notes are not detailed – they are for guidance only and should be used in conjunction with the appropriate maps. (The entire route is covered by the Ordnance Survey's Explorer sheets OL4, OL5, OL6 and OL7, as well as by Harvey's four Superwalker maps covering the National Park.) The journey is rough and pathless in a few places and often ventures on to the high fells, so anyone attempting it should know their own limitations and be fully prepared for the hills.

GPX TRACKS

GPX tracks for the route in this book are available to download free at www.cicerone.co.uk/1087/GPX. A GPS device is an excellent aid to navigation, but you should also carry a map and compass and know how to use them. GPX files are provided in good faith, but neither the author nor the publisher accept responsibility for their accuracy.

CHAPTER 1
Loweswater to Ennerdale
(Loweswater, Crummock Water, Buttermere)

Lakeland's high fells are still slumbering beneath a light summer blanket of cloud as the lithe Wasdale farmer leaps from the car and walks down to the shores of Loweswater. It's five o'clock in the morning – that soft, slightly sombre time, just before the sun reaches the valley bottoms, but there's already a sense of promise in the air. This will be a special day. The grazing sheep don't realise this; they don't even look up as the man passes through their meadow and crouches to touch the water. How would they know? There's no fanfare. Not even a photographer from the local newspaper to capture the moment when legendary fell-runner Joss Naylor embarks on his attempt to break yet another long-distance record. Yet this is a day that will live on in fell-running lore, and one that Joss himself will remember as among the finest in his life…

This is a day that will live on in fell-running lore

The day was 25 June 1983, and Loweswater was the starting point for a 105-mile (169km) journey, with almost 20,000ft (6098m) of ascent, that would see Joss visit 27 of Lakeland's largest bodies of water, the so-called Lakes, Meres and Waters (LMW), in 19hr 14min. 'It's a lot tougher than people are aware,' Joss explains as we retrace his steps almost exactly 37 years later. 'The shorter course – without doing Kentmere twice – there's only a dozen done it, if that. I don't know why, because it's a beautiful thing to do. I took a lot in that day and, when I finished, I felt I'd achieved summat very special. Maybe it's just beyond the ordinary runner – it's a big step up from the Bob Graham; all that extra mileage.'

As we set off on 24 June 2020, the sheep seem just as uninterested as they did in 1983. With the heat already building, Joss – wearing shorts, baseball cap and sunglasses – notes that the weather conditions are also similar to those of 37 years earlier. Aside from the early fell-top mist, some disorientating low cloud near Haycock and a spot of drizzle late in the day at Keswick, it had been a warm, sunny day with temperatures getting up to about 20°C. Joss, having touched the water, turns his back on Loweswater and we're off, making our way through the western valleys at a fast walking pace.

◀ Looking down on Loweswater, with Grasmoor and Crummock Water in the distance

◀ Early morning, 25 June 1983, and Joss makes his way down to the shores of Loweswater (Photo credit: Dave Elliott)

Joss turns his back on Loweswater and we're off

▲ Touching Loweswater in 2020

Whiteside's scree slopes and the dramatic, gully-ridden western face of Grasmoor dominate the scene ahead, while dark Mellbreak stands aloof to the south. The next lake, Crummock Water, puts in an appearance too as we stand beside the village hall, watching house martins dart in and out of its porch. 'It's good to see the swallows and house martins,' says Joss. 'There's two house martins landed at ours about 10 days ago. They built a nest. They're late coming this year – about two or three weeks behind – but the swallows were early.' He tells of how one neighbour, several years ago, had about 20 nests removed because the birds were leaving their droppings on his window ledges. 'Summat like that nettles me; the birds were doing no harm.'

The driver of a United Utilities van pulls up and winds his window down to say hello. It turns out to be Carl Bell, of Keswick Athletic Club, the current British and English men's fell-running champion. 'They're like London buses,' laughs photographer Stephen Wilson. 'You go out with one fell-running legend and another turns up out of the blue.' This is the first of dozens of similar encounters throughout the Lakes over the course of the summer where we bump into Joss's friends, acquaintances and admirers. Fell-runners, walkers, farmers, forestry workers…many want to stop and chat, and Joss, always generous, has time for them all. A spark of friendly recognition in the eyes of others – sometimes shy, sometimes uncertain – confirms we're in the presence of Lakeland royalty: the King of the Fells.

Beyond that icon of Lakeland pubs, the Kirkstile Inn, the route follows a series of walled lonnings. These ancient lanes and pathways criss-cross Cumbria, connecting many of the county's settlements. While a few, now swamped by brambles and bracken, are impassable, most are still public rights of way that are regularly used. 'Aye! They're lovely, these old lanes,' exclaims Joss as he stops on Park Bridge to admire the stonework. It doesn't matter that he's not on the fells; he's clearly enjoying everything around him, every little detail – the walls, the cottages, the wildlife…

Passing beneath Mellbreak's northern crags, we skirt the edge of Green Wood. It lives up to its name today, sumptuously verdant in the middle of summer. Come winter though, the oaks' bare, gnarly branches take on a more sinister appearance, reaching out like withered limbs to passing walkers and runners. These aren't the grand, towering, pedunculate oaks associated with the English lowlands, but smaller sessile oaks, typical of upland areas with high rainfall and acidic soils, particularly in the north and west of Britain. Once upon a time, these trees, draped with beard lichens, would have formed an immense forest that cloaked the whole of Europe's Atlantic coast – all the way from Portugal to Norway. 'There's some

▲ Summer in the western valleys

ancient ones there,' says Joss, indicating the oaks. 'There's a massive one on Irton Pike, down by Parkgate Tarn. Tremendous girth on it.' Both awe and respect are clearly evident in his tone.

A path of close-cropped turf leads away from the trees and then down to the edge of Crummock Water. 'There's a bit of bounce now that the ground's not so hard; the rain's softened it without making it too wet,' notes Joss. He recalls how, on his LMW run, he came thundering down this slope and couldn't apply the brakes fast enough; he ended up almost ankle deep in the lake. This time, he manages to stop at the shore. He stands quietly for a few seconds, looking across to Grasmoor and then says: 'That's lovely, in't it?' No fancy words; just a moment of simple, heartfelt connection with the surrounding scenery.

It is a moment of simple, heartfelt connection with the surrounding scenery

And that scenery grows in grandeur as the route makes its way south along the western shores of Crummock Water. All focus is on the ground for the first few hundred yards, as the waterlogged peat threatens to suck shoes from feet that err. Beyond that though, it's the fells that command attention. In her essay 'The Lake District' written in the middle of the 19th century while on a tour of the Lakes, the social theorist Harriet Martineau described Crummock Water as 'less celebrated among the lakes than its peculiarities and beauties appear to deserve'. The same is true today, as tourists drive past it, giving it only a cursory glance as they hurry on for Instagrammable images of its more famous neighbour, Buttermere. 'From stations on its rocky and elevated shores the most striking views are obtained of the noble surrounding mountains...' wrote Martineau of Crummock.

▲ Crummock Water

Immediately above the lakeside path, grass slopes quickly give way to steeper, rockier ground that leads to the 1680ft (512m) summit of Mellbreak. On the other side of the water, Grasmoor again, its vertiginous arêtes and dark gullies looking impenetrable from this angle. (Yet you can almost guarantee, on a dry, calm summer's day like this, there will be an adventurous few making their painstaking way up Lorton Gully, a grade-three scramble that cuts into the mountain's western face.) Up ahead, to the south, the Buttermere fells close in as if guarding a gem or concealing a secret.

Joss disturbed a small gaggle of geese as he ran, solo, along these shores in 1983. 'There were about half a dozen of 'em on the ground beside the lake. I was a bit surprised to see 'em because that's not typical grazing ground for geese – you normally see 'em in fields. But as I came near, they took off and settled on the lake.'

The going becomes soggy again as the route crosses flatter ground where Scale Beck enters the lake. Upstream, but out of sight from the shore path, is Scale Force, Lakeland's longest waterfall. Hidden away in a narrow ravine, it consists of several slender drops which, when added together, fall a total of about 170ft. A few weeks earlier, and Joss would've been able to see Rannerdale, bathed in its annual bluebell glory, on the far side of the water. By late June though, the wildflowers had wilted and lost their radiance.

We rest for a while on the tiny humpback bridge that spans Buttermere Dubs, the short beck that connects Buttermere and Crummock Water. At the end of the last glacial period, the two lakes were one and this area would have been under water. It's only as the becks, pouring off the fells, deposited their loads of rocks and soil that this new, fertile land formed. For us, it's a chance to rest and take stock before heading up those water-scoured slopes for the first big climb on the route – up past Bleaberry Tarn and on to Red Pike. It's a punishing ascent, gaining more than 2000ft (600m) in altitude in just 1.3 miles (2.2km). With more than 100 miles to go, putting a climb like that into your legs so early on would be unthinkable for many runners. 'I never really thought about how hard it was,' Joss says, looking up at the wooded slopes. 'You've just got to be running right. You can soon lose five or ten minutes on a climb like that if you're not running right. You start off with short strides while your body adjusts and then you put the pressure on, lengthening your stride. You'll go that la'al bit faster.'

There would've been no apprehension about the long day ahead beyond this big climb, then? 'No, you just get on with it. Concentrate on the next section you're doing, and don't go beyond that. You put things together as you go along. And you put pain to the back of your mind.'

Before Red Pike though, the route pays a visit to what Joss describes as the 'most picturesque bit of water in the Lake District' – Buttermere. 'There's summat magic about it. This la'al valley has got summat very, very special when you catch it on the right day. When I did my 70 at 70, I stopped on top of Hay Stacks and you could see every detail in Buttermere. The lake itself was beyond a looking glass, it was so sharp; it was sharper in the water than it was out. It was just the right time, the right light. I sat down for a couple of minutes, just took it in.'

The '70 at 70' to which Joss refers is just one of the many seemingly superhuman runs that he has completed – this one involving 70 Lakeland tops spread over a distance of more than 50 miles (80km) with more than 25,000ft (7620m) of ascent. All achieved in less than 21 hours on 5 July 2006, just months after his 70th birthday.

At the age of 47 though, his LMW attempt had only just begun. The checkpoint marshal Ian Richardson recorded him dipping his hands in Buttermere at 05:37, already five minutes ahead of schedule. He stood and paused – barely long enough to take in the mountains jealously guarding this beautiful spot – to gaze up at Fleetwith Edge, the fine shoulder of rock rising unerringly heavenward from the opposite end of the lake. Then he was off again.

> The 'most picturesque bit of water in the Lake District' – Buttermere

From Buttermere, the route climbs, first through the forest and then up open slopes. The gradient briefly eases as the well-walked path nears the corrie. Now, the bucolic niceties of the lowland pubs and lonnings are forgotten as the mountains draw ever closer. The headwall looks formidable – Chapel Crags straight ahead, rising in an arc to the dark buttresses of High Stile, while the still waters of Bleaberry Tarn sit sullenly at their feet. Our way goes off to the west though, up to The Saddle before tackling the haematite-stained screes of Red Pike itself. One final pull and Joss reaches the bare, stony summit – at 2476ft (755m), one of the highest points on the entire route.

Red Pike is part of a procession of high tops that splits the Buttermere valley from Ennerdale. As part of that ridge, it marks the point at which the moody moorland to the north-west gives way to the rockier, more mountainous terrain leading up and over High Stile and High Crag. From this vantage point, Joss could look back down on Crummock Water and Buttermere. The fell views are expansive too, taking in all of the major groups apart from the Coniston Fells. They're all there – Scafell Pike, Great Gable, Skiddaw, even Helvellyn and High Street far to the east...

▲ Resting above Buttermere on the way up to Red Pike

'I was climbing well,' Joss recalls in his typically understated way. From Red Pike's summit, he explains, he would've descended into Ennerdale on a good path through the trees. 'You'd drop in at the top of the lake, but that path's gone now. Last time I was there, it was full of briars and you couldn't use it. Now you have to drop down on to the forest road itself. Things alter.' Today, the best way into Ennerdale from Red Pike is to follow the high-level alternative of Wainwright's long-distance walk that links St Bees on the Irish Sea coast with the North Sea fishing village of Robin Hood's Bay. While most Coast to Coasters keep to the valley route through Ennerdale, enough of them climb Red Pike's south-western slopes to have worn a path through the heather.

▲ Buttermere was the third body of water on the run (Photo credit: Dave Elliott)

▲ The Wild Ennerdale project began in 2003

Nearing the valley bottom, the rough, spiky grass – what Joss calls 'benty grass' – hides numerous lumps and bumps spread over the landscape. Some are natural but many are of human construct – prehistoric cairnfields as well as the remains of longhouses and cultivation terraces dating back to medieval times. Back then, this part of Ennerdale, known as Gillerthwaite, would have been home to a small community of pastoralists. Today, it's better known as being home to one of this remote dale's two hostels – and, thanks to Wild Ennerdale, one of the richest, most diverse natural habitats in the Lake District.

The Wild Ennerdale project began in 2003 when the valley's three main landowners – the National Trust, the Forestry Commission (now Forestry England) and United Utilities – decided to embark on an ambitious scheme that would return the area to a more 'natural' state. The partners' vision is 'to allow the evolution of Ennerdale as a wild valley for the benefit of people, relying more

It is one of the richest, most diverse natural habitats in the Lake District

on natural processes to shape its landscape and ecology'. Nowhere is this lack of human interference more evident than in the meandering River Liza. Probably one of the most natural rivers in England, it is not constrained in any way. In fact, when the river changed course in autumn storms a few years ago and overwhelmed a public right of way, a decision was made not to divert the new channel but to divert the path instead.

Semi-wild Galloway cattle roam freely in the valley. They were introduced in 2006 when ecologists advised the Wild Ennerdale team that the grazing and disturbance caused by large herbivores, largely absent from British forests, was necessary to open the way for different plant species. Like everything else in the valley, they are mostly left to their own devices. Calves are born unaided – the mother going off to a secluded place to give birth and then returning to the herd a few days later.

As a result of these management decisions, biodiversity is benefitting. The valley and the surrounding fells are now home to more than 100 species of bird; the endangered red squirrel maintains one of its last English bastions here; and, following a reintroduction programme, England's largest population of the rare marsh fritillary butterfly thrives here. Joss recalls standing on a bridge over Smithy Beck, close to where it feeds into Ennerdale Water, and watching five pairs of one of the rarest fish species in Britain, the Arctic char, heading upstream. They had been on the brink of extinction, but the numbers spawning in Ennerdale increased from just a handful to more than 500 within three years of the creation of a hatchery and the dismantling of pipe bridges. 'Only time I've ever seen 'em,' says Joss. 'They were probably going upstream to spawn.'

We rest for a while on logs beside the forest road, listening to the birds, admiring the amazing fell scenery. At the head of the valley looms the massive, scree-girted dome of Great Gable, while, on the other side of the River Liza, the ground rises abruptly to the peaks of Haycock, Steeple and Pillar. Pillar Rock, a formidable tower on the north face of its parent fell, is supposedly where the sport of rock-climbing was born. Local man John Atkinson first scaled the rock in 1826, and the first 'tourist' to climb it, a Royal Navy lieutenant by the name of Wilson, followed 22 years later. Even today, climbers come here to test their mettle on a complex crag that is home to many classic routes of varying degrees of difficulty. While we absorb this landscape, both dramatic and historic, Joss remains standing. It's clear that, even in his mid 80s, he's not used to being still for long periods of time. 'Come on, then. Let's go and look at this lake!' As the rest of us slowly gather our things together, Joss is off again...

> At the head of the valley looms the massive, scree-girted dome of Great Gable

▲ Stage 1 ends in Ennerdale

DAVE'S STORY

Dave Elliott was apprentice instructor at Sellafield at the time Joss was working there in the early 1980s. He gathered a team of volunteers, all Sellafield apprentices and Duke of Edinburgh Award candidates, to act as marshals along the route of Joss's 1983 run. 'The idea was to have at least two people at each lake, mere and water,' says Dave. 'They all had to synchronise their watches with the "speaking clock" before they left home in the morning to get the accurate split times.' Some of the apprentices also joined Joss on sections of the run, as did Sellafield instructor Alan Jackman.

Dave, incidentally, was also the man who, in the absence of a press photographer, took all the photos of the LMW used in this book. He used a black-and-white film at the request of the local newspapers. (It was still a few years before most newspapers would move to using colour photography.)

Soon after Dave dropped Joss off at Loweswater, he met up with other members of the support team in the car park at Buttermere.

'It was about five o'clock in the morning. There must've been two or three vehicles there, support people – people who were there to help with food and drinks, massages, equipment changes plus any strapping or medication that may have been required.' They were all eager and excited; the anticipation of this day had been building for weeks.

'It was a lovely morning and we were chatting away, not realising the time of day. Then this rather well-spoken chap stuck his head out of a window of one of the rooms in the pub and waved us over. "Excuse me. Have you got a moment, please?" Very polite, like. So I walked across and said, "Morning, can I help you?" He barked back, "Yes! You can eff off! We're trying to get some sleep here." We'd forgotten that, while Joss was out running and we were doing our bit to help him, most other people were still sleeping. We left immediately, apologising as we did.'

STAGE 1

Start Roadside parking opposite driveway to Askill and Miresyke at Waterend, Loweswater (NY 118 224)

Finish YHA Ennerdale, Gillerthwaite, Ennerdale (NY 142 141)

Distance 9.1 miles (14.7km)

Ascent 2710ft (826m)

Approximate walking time 5hr–5hr 30min

▶ Go through the pedestrian gate at the western end of the lay-by. Cross two meadows to a lane and turn left. Two gates mark the end of the lane just after the farmhouse at **Hudson Place**; go through the left-hand one. Follow the track into **Holme Wood** and then turn left along a surfaced path to reach the southern shore of **Loweswater**. Rejoin the main woodland track just beyond the stone-built bunkhouse. Beyond the trees, the track passes **Watergate Farm** and climbs to the road. Turn right.

▶ Turn right after the village hall. Turn right at the pub and keep left as the lane immediately splits. Take the next lane on the right. Keep left after crossing Park Bridge. The lane, rougher now, ends at a gate. Go through, follow the grassy track for about 35 metres and then swing up to the right, through a gate in the wall. You'll soon join a clear path along the edge of Green Wood. Beyond the trees, keep following the line of the wall on the left – down to the shores of **Crummock Water**. Head south, with the lake on your left. (The path is peaty and indistinct beyond the bridges crossing the two arms of Scale Beck; simply stay parallel with the lake.)

▶ A stony path continues beyond the southern tip of Crummock Water to reach the north-western end of **Buttermere**. Cross the wooden bridge over Sourmilk Gill and, in a few more metres, take the path on the right heading steeply uphill through the trees. Beyond the forest, this climbs to **Bleaberry Tarn** and then continues, on an increasingly eroded path, to the top of **Red Pike**.

▶ Head south-west, soon picking up a faint path, cairned in places, descending Red Pike's southern slopes. After fording Gillflinter Beck, the trail descends between two arms of the forest to reach the valley track in **Ennerdale**. Turn right, reaching the YHA hostel at **Gillerthwaite** in 320 metres.

▲ Bridge over Sourmilk Gill

Chapter 1 – Loweswater to Ennerdale   31

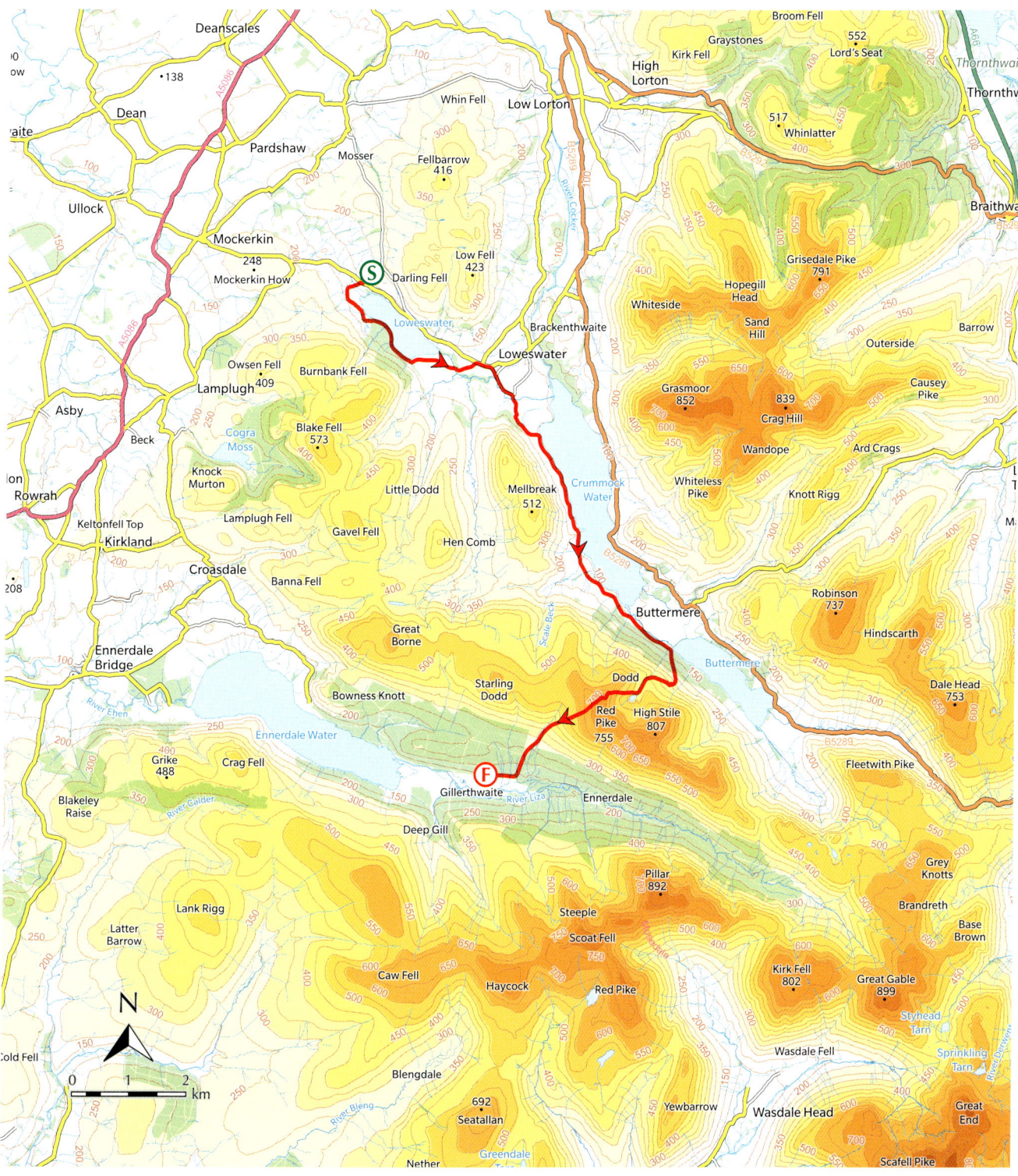

CHAPTER 2
Ennerdale to Eskdale Green
(Ennerdale Water, Wastwater)

The rapid click-clacking sound of Joss's poles on the ground accompanies us as we hot-foot it along the forest road through Ennerdale. There's no need to rush – we're in no great hurry and it's midsummer, so there's plenty of daylight – but Joss doesn't hang around. Decades of constant movement are ingrained in his DNA and, even at the age of 84, there's not much sign of him slowing down. The poles are one of his few concessions to growing old. He began using them about 10 years ago at the suggestion of 'the management', his wife, Mary. 'They make a big difference,' he says. 'They tek the weight off me knees.' I suggest they help steady him too. 'Aye,' he replies, straight-faced, 'you can have an extra pint.'

I later realise that, after the relatively relaxed start at Loweswater, he's clicked into training mode in Ennerdale. He's on record as saying that forestry roads are great for runners looking to improve their performance and that, if you can run well on their uneven, unpredictable surfaces, you can run well anywhere. 'I used to bring Brasher and his marathon men down here,' he later tells me, referring to his friend, athlete and co-founder of the London Marathon, Chris Brasher. 'It's slightly downhill from Black Sail and they used to leg it, like.'

We're almost on home turf for Joss now

We're almost on home turf for Joss now. He started shepherding in this valley as a child, crossing from his family's farm in neighbouring Wasdale on a regular basis. 'I used to put some hard days in over here. I used to gather those forests out from when I left school. I'd gather for all sorts of people back then – through till Moses Trod on Ennerdale side, drop in back of Black Sail Hut; out till Brandreth, Green Gable and the Westmorland Cairn. There were only odd 'uns up there though. Scamp, one of me dogs, used to go up the gill till Sprinkling Tarn, down till Styhead Tarn. The old dog knew where to go. Lassie used to go on the other side. I had another dog called Patch, with a lot of bark.'

He says he knew 'every crag' in Ennerdale. 'Willie told me all their names.' Willie Monkhouse worked for Joss's father, Joe, and it

◀ Wastwater from Yewbarrow, with Bowderdale to the right

was Willie who first brought Joss into Ennerdale when he was just eight or nine years old. 'I went with him, but I remember him saying, "It's mebbe too far for those la'al legs to go"'. While Scott, Joss's eldest brother, was gathering, Willie and the young shepherd-in-waiting walked to the other side of Pillar Rock. '"I'll show you summat," Willie said to me. And it was the view right down to the end of the lake. He says, "This is what I call Bonny Corner. It's the best view of Ennerdale you can see from anywhere."'

And what a view! The narrow, glacier-carved valley, hemmed in on both sides by high fells, with the forest reaching right down to the water's edge in places. It's changed little since then. The forest is still there, although the sterile, regimented conifer plantations planted from the 1920s onwards are steadily being replaced by the richer array of species associated with native woodland. The dale also remains one of the few Lakeland valleys without a road running through it, lending it a tremendous sense of isolation and remoteness. Light pollution is practically unknown here, the Milky Way putting in regular appearances on cloudless nights.

The lake itself, Ennerdale Water, is the eighth largest in the National Park, covering a surface area of 768 acres (300 hectares). Although it is a natural feature, for about 120 years it has been the source of drinking water for the people of Whitehaven, but abstraction is due to end in 2022.

By the time Joss dipped his hands in it on his LMW run, he was already 29 minutes ahead of schedule. It was also here that he was joined by the first of his pacemakers, John Wild. An instructor at RAF Cosford in Shropshire, John ran for England in cross-country and steeplechase events and, at the time of writing, still holds the course records for four British fell races. 'He was a serious runner; he didn't stop to turn stones over,' Joss recalls. 'He and Kenny Stuart had some great battles.'

From the lake shore, Joss and John headed into the dark forest, climbing beside Woundell Beck and then Deep Gill. Even by Ennerdale standards, this is a secretive little side valley. Few would've visited it back in 1983, and few visit it today. The oppressiveness normally associated with conifer plantations, where the silence can sometimes be overwhelming, is thankfully absent here. The melodious song of wrens and tits and willow warblers is accompanied by the background percussion of the beck, bringing the place alive. Only as the runners drew parallel with a small waterfall would the roar of the water have drowned out everything else.

Beyond a gate and stile on the forest edge, the heather-covered slopes ahead steepen, closing in on the beck. Today, the faint trail runs out early, and those aiming for the high ridge are better off climbing on to Tewit How and following the route of a little-used bridleway along the crest of this broad spur. In 1983 though, Joss continued right up Deep Gill, along a trod where, for decades, he'd gathered sheep. 'The way I went that morning, it was runnable. The path was on the ground back then, but since the sheep've gone, it's grown over. When you've got 300 or 400 sheep going up, they soon create a path, but I went up there a couple of years ago and it's thick heather. Never again! There's a good alternative for anybody going out now though – there's a la'al path, in the heather there, that goes past Tewit How Tarn.'

Joss's original route took him up into the lonely bowl of Great Cove on the north face of Haycock. 'The ground's clearer here, but it has odd little knotty crags.' A short pull then led on to the main ridge where, within three miles of his Bowderdale home, Joss suffered his only navigational error of the day. 'We went over the saddle between Haycock and Scoat into thick, black mist. I remember saying to John, "We'll have to concentrate. One wrong turn and we'll be lost." But we had a lot to talk about, so I wasn't concentrating. Back then, there were three sheep paths through here. If I'd dropped on to the second path, I'd have been all right.' Instead, he veered too far west and began, unknowingly, to head into the upper reaches of Blengdale, the place he describes as the quietest in all of Lakeland. 'If it's thick mist like that and it's featureless, everything looks the same. When I got to the spring though, I knew, and shot back. Once we come off Seatallan end, the mist cleared again and, after that, it was a decent day right up till we came into Keswick.'

And what was the topic of conversation that almost led to disaster for Joss's record attempt? Nothing much, according to John, nearly four decades later. 'It was just blokes talking together   rubbish as normal probably.'

Beyond the pools at the evocatively named Pots of Ashness and the boggy ground between Middle Fell and Seatallan, the route drops past Greendale Tarn to begin its descent into Wasdale, with The Screes soon appearing on the other side of Wastwater. Aside from the winters he now spends in the warmer climes of southern Spain – to ease circulatory problems – Joss has been proud to call this glorious valley his home all his life. The farming community at Wasdale Head is where his story began – born at Middle Row Farm, at the foot of England's highest mountains. As an independent adult, he farmed at Bowderdale for 37 years, just up from the shores of Wastwater, England's deepest lake. His son Paul eventually took over there, while Joss shifted down valley to Greendale, before moving to the village of Gosforth, at the mouth of Wasdale, in 2018.

The farming community at Wasdale Head is where his story began

Looking across Ennerdale Water to Bowness Knott ▶

▲ Bowderdale sits between Middle Fell (left) and the shapely Yewbarrow

Chapter 2 – Ennerdale to Eskdale Green   37

That's three moves, covering a total distance of just nine miles, over the course of more than 80 years.

Crossing the farmland between Greendale and the lake, Joss finds time, on our rewalk of the route, to detour to the top of a knoll. Like the king of the castle, he peruses the landscape and admits that, on every run he ever did, there was always 'summat very special' about entering his home valley – even if, as when he was doing the LMW, he wasn't going to stop for long.

With rain threatening, we walk along a darkening, tree-shrouded lane, the dank verdancy bringing an eerie beauty to the spot. Creeping, curling fronds of maidenhair spleenwort grow from the high wall on one side. Joss admires the craftsmanship that's gone into building the wall and tells of how there used to be a terraced garden behind it – a bit like in *The Secret Garden* – until the owner decided he'd make some money by growing Christmas trees on the land.

'I've seen some fantastic reflections in Wastwater'

Our next glimpse of Wastwater, seen from the path down to the YHA hostel, is a little surreal. For a split second, it seems as if we're higher than we are, and are looking down into a steep-sided, rocky canyon. In fact, what we're seeing is The Screes immaculately mirrored on the calm surface of the water. The dividing line between the ground and its reflection is impossible to make out. Later, looking back up the lake from its south-western end, the outline of Yewbarrow is near perfect – only an almost imperceptible shimmering movement along its outline reveals it to be a reflection.

'I've seen some fantastic reflections in Wastwater,' Joss reminisces. 'One day, I turned the corner where the boathouse is, and there was a picture there of Gable as if it'd been dropped in the lake. Every detail was there – Gable was covered in snow and the clouds above it were pitch black. The water looked evil. I went home to get me camera, came back and it were gone. It was there once; I've never seen anything like it since. It was unreal.'

He continues: 'Then there was this one night I went round the lake. It'd been one of those days when it'd rained and stormed all day and then it'd cleared out; Nether Beck and Over Beck were running white, and everything else round about was green. There were just these two white lines coming into the lake. It's all about getting the right light.'

Tales of almost spiritual encounters with the lake give way to reflections on its darker side. Joss recalls the discovery of the

▲ 'I've seen some fantastic reflections in Wastwater'

almost perfectly preserved body of Margaret Hogg in 1984. Her husband had killed her eight years earlier and dumped her body in Wastwater but, due to the lack of oxygen in the water, a wax-like substance had encased her, making the job of identification – and subsequent prosecution – relatively easy.

Margaret's body was only found by accident, as divers trawled the lake for missing French backpacker, Véronique Marre. Joss has a story about her disappearance too, remembering how he told a police officer looking for her that they needed to conduct a thorough search of The Screes, an area of massive, unstable boulders along the lake's south-eastern edge where walkers often come a cropper. 'He told me a helicopter had already searched that area,' he recalls, rolling his eyes as if to say, 'A helicopter's not going to find a body among The Screes'. And that's exactly where the French student's body did eventually turn up, among the shattered rocks at the foot of Broken Rib Crag, several weeks after the grisly discovery of Margaret Hogg's corpse.

The sudden appearance of a sandpiper puts a welcome end to these dark recollections. A high-pitched tweeping accompanies its skilful aerial manoeuvres as it skims the surface of the lake, as close to the water as a darting swift. Joss comments that he once saw a kingfisher nearby, but it was the only one he ever saw in Wasdale.

The path skirts the edge of the elegant Low Wood, briefly running alongside the River Irt as it drains Wastwater. Unlike Joss's 1983 round, which was completed in less than a day, our 2020 journey is spread over several weeks and the weather has already taken a dramatic turn since our scorching start at Loweswater. There have been some massive downpours, including eight inches of rain in one day, so the Irt is in a tumultuous hurry to reach the Irish Sea, more than 13 meandering miles away.

On the trail above the farm at Easthwaite, I walk directly behind Joss, watching how his feet nimbly negotiate the roughest, rockiest sections. At first, I think I'm imagining it, but repeated observations confirm that, instead of slowing down as most people would on encountering tricky bits, Joss performs a little 'dance' – his feet, indeed the whole of his lower body, moving like that of a person less than half his age.

He leads us into the forests around Latterbarrow, just beneath Irton Fell, deciding we should keep as true to his original line as possible – a corner is cut by using a partially waterlogged firebreak. I hear a splash behind me as one of our companions goes in up to his knee. Swearing ensues.

'Whose idea was this?' calls Joss from the front of the line.

'Yours, Joss!' goes the chorus behind.

A deer, startled by the commotion, shoots from the trees just ahead of us, its white rump blinking on and off as it flashes

> His feet nimbly negotiate the roughest, rockiest sections

▲ Joss leads us into the forests around Latterbarrow

through the undergrowth and then vanishes almost as quickly as it appeared.

Emerging from the forest, the route crosses damp ground where the star-shaped, yellow flowers of bog asphodel thrive. Later in the year, the plant will turn orange, adding to the kaleidoscope of deeper, richer hues that brings a fresh dimension of colour to the fells in the autumn. For now though, summer prevails, as the bracken and the grasses clothing the north-facing slopes of Irton Fell sport their brightest greens. From the top of the low ridge, there's a temptation to head on to Whin Rigg to the north, and teeter along the top of the precipitous cliffs overlooking Wastwater, but there's no chance for such exhilarating deviations on the route of Joss's LMW. Instead, there's just enough time to get your breath back before plunging straight down the other side into the forests of Miterdale. We cross the River Mite before one short pull along an old lane leads into Eskdale proper.

Forestry England's Giggle Alley plantation lies to the north of the lane, hiding another 'secret garden'. This one appears to have a finer pedigree than the one at High Scale, near Wastwater, having been designed in 1914 by a team led by the renowned landscape architect Thomas Mawson. Recently restored, some of the many exotic features of the so-called Japanese Garden include bamboo thickets, maples, magnolia and azaleas. In 1983 though, it remained overgrown and largely forgotten. Joss would've been unaware of it as his feet hit the asphalt at Eskdale Green and he began his first stretch of road running since Loweswater.

> Summer prevails, as the bracken and the grasses sport their brightest greens

ENNERDALE HORSESHOE FELL RACE

The Ennerdale Horseshoe has long been one of Joss's favourite fell races. The event was set up in 1968 by Joe Long and Frank Travis, of the West Cumberland Orienteering Club, and is now organised by the Cumberland Fell Runners Association. The course is just less than 23 miles long (36.8km) with a whopping total of 7510ft (2290m) of ascent, taking in Great Borne, Red Pike, the High Stile ridge, Hay Stacks, Green Gable, Kirk Fell, Pillar, Haycock and Crag Fell. At the time of writing, the men's course record was 3hr 20min 57sec, set by Kenny Stuart in 1984, while Janet McIver set the women's record in 2008 with a time of 4hr 1min 33sec.

Joss won the first nine runs – from 1968 to 1976 – and competed almost every year for a total of 30 years, only missing the 1977 event due to injury. His best time was in 1972, when he completed the course in 3hr 30min 40sec. His last win, when he set a course record for veterans over 40, coincided with the announcement that he was to receive the MBE for services to fell-running. After 1998, he competed on an occasional basis, his last run being in 2006 when he ran the route as a veteran over 70, completing it in 6hr 37min 15sec. He still attends the event, signing certificates and presenting prizes. Sometimes, he heads on to the fells to pass out drinks and words of encouragement to the runners.

▶ Flashback to the start of the Ennerdale Horseshoe, early 1970s (Photo from Joss's own collection; photographer unknown)

▲ Joss was born at Middle Row Farm, Wasdale Head

A WASDALE CHILDHOOD

The youngest child of Joseph and Ella Naylor, Joss was born on 10 February 1936 at Middle Row Farm, Wasdale Head – close to the foot of England's highest and most rugged mountains. His parents had previously farmed at Fellside, near Caldbeck, on the Lake District's Northern Fells, but moved to the western Lakes in 1926. Joss went to school at the mouth of the remote dale, in Gosforth, the village where, in his mid 80s, he now lives.

As in all farming families, the young Joss and his three siblings – James, Scott and Marjorie – had jobs to do before and after school, including caring for the hens, milking the cows, raking hay and shovelling coal. They would sometimes have to give up their beds for paying guests – often climbers wanting to take on Wasdale's imposing crags – and, on these occasions, would sleep in wooden huts on the farm. It wasn't an easy life, and it was one that was made even harder by a back injury that has plagued him almost his entire life, but Joss loved being on the farm and on the surrounding fells. There was never any doubt that he'd leave school at 15 to work on the farm. He eventually took on his own tenancy, just a couple of miles down the valley at the more remote Bowderdale, just after marrying Mary in early 1963.

One of Joss's earliest memories is of being shown the power that natural forces can exert when you live in a place such as Wasdale Head. He remembers being taken, at the age of three, to see the damage that had been done by a flash flood down Lingmell Gill, one of the main becks feeding from the Scafell group into the top end of Wastwater. 'The prisoners of war, from the 14–18 war, had put a wall each side of the river and paved the bottom of it from just above the lake till beyond Brackenclose,' he recalls. 'It took them years to put in – it'd been an absolute showpiece – but that big flood of 1939 washed it all out in just one night. There wasn't a sign of it left after that. It's just unbelievable what the power of water can do in the Lake District.'

STAGE 2

Start YHA Ennerdale, Gillerthwaite, Ennerdale (NY 142 141)

Finish Forestry England's Giggle Alley car park, Eskdale Green (NY 141 002)

Distance 12.2 miles (19.6km)

Ascent 3160ft (963m)

Approximate walking time 6hr 30min–7hr 30min

▶ Head west along the forest road for 0.7 miles (1.1km) and then turn left to cross the bridge over Char Dub (**River Liza**). After briefly detouring right to touch **Ennerdale Water**, go through the gate into the forest at the southern end of the track and turn left. About 200 metres after the bridge over **Woundell Beck** – and just before a gate across the track – there are two paths on the right. Ignore the one heading steeply uphill through the firebreak; instead, take the track ascending south-west through the trees.

▶ Beyond the small gate at the forest edge, follow Deep Gill upstream for a further 240 metres, ford a tributary beck and then follow this upstream. The trail, obscured by heather and bracken, is hard to make out. Having followed it for 160 metres, contour south for just 25 metres and then swing up the steep slope again. The trail runs parallel with the tributary gill, through choking heather at first and then across easier ground. Almost 455 metres after parting company with Deep Gill, join a clearer path heading south-east on to **Tewit How**. From the cairn, head south-south-east into the saddle between **Haycock** and **Scoat Fell**.

▶ Join the bridleway dropping south-south-east. After 550 metres, as the descent steepens again, veer south-west (away from Nether Beck) on a faint, intermittent path around Haycock's southern flanks. Nearing the **Pots of Ashness**, the ground starts rising towards **Seatallan**. Leave the rising path here and head south-east, across pathless, tussocky ground on the fell's eastern slopes. Locate a path skirting the rock outcrops of Winscale Hows. Follow this to the marshy ground at the head of the beck feeding into **Greendale Tarn**. Descend beside the tarn's western shore, cross the outlet stream and then follow the beck downstream. After joining the path from **Middle Fell**, you reach a fork. Bear right, with the walls of **Greendale** on your left. Reach the road where the beck passes under it.

▶ Pick up the bridleway heading into Roan Wood on the south-western side of the bridge over Greendale Gill. Leaving the trees, head south-west across open, damp ground. About 135 metres after the next gate, bear left along an old track. This heads south-east at first, but then swings north-east to reach a gate and ladder stile. Follow the track to the road. Go left and, almost immediately, through a small gate on the right. A permissive path leads down to YHA Wasdale Hall. Drop to the shore of **Wastwater** and turn right, keeping the water (the lake and then the River Irt) on your left for 0.7 miles (1.1km).

▶ Leaving Low Wood, bear left to cross Lund Bridge over the River Irt. Follow the river upstream, the trail eventually coming out on to a vehicle-wide track. Turn right and, in 100 metres, go through the gate on the left. Head roughly south, rising to a gate in the top wall. Once through this, turn right. After fording **Greathall Gill**, keep following the rough path as it skirts the bracken-covered fellside. Maintaining height, keep left on nearing the farm at **Easthwaite**, soon joining a broad path heading uphill. A gate leads into the **Latterbarrow** forest. Keep to the forest edge for 310 metres and then turn sharp left along a more solid track. After the path swings slightly right beyond wooden railings, make sure you swing left to pass between another set of railings on a rising stony path.

▶ Beyond the forest, the trail climbs the open fellside. On the high ground of **Irton Fell**, go through the gate in the old forest boundary. Follow the bridleway down to the **River Mite**, crossing several broad forest tracks along the way. Beyond the river, cross the **Miterdale** lane to join the broad track opposite. Known as Smithybrow Lane, this drops to Forestry England's Giggle Alley parking area at **Eskdale Green**.

Chapter 2 – Ennerdale to Eskdale Green   43

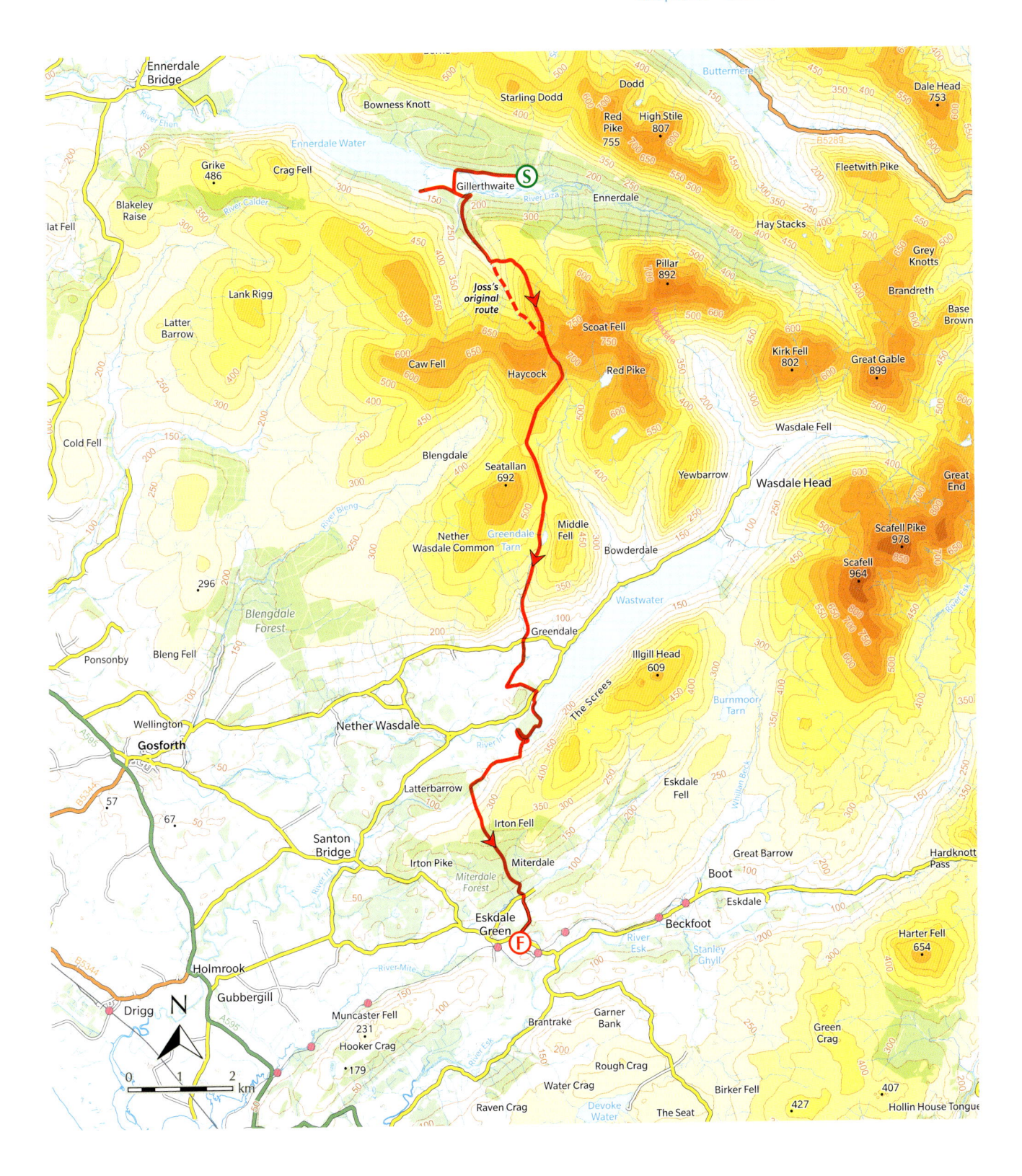

CHAPTER 3
Eskdale Green to Dunnerdale
(Devoke Water)

'It's gonna rain.' There's barely a cloud in the sky as we set off from Eskdale, and there's no rain forecast. I look at Joss. Sometimes, he'll give you a little sideways glance or there'll be a glint in his eyes, revealing another of his gentle wind-ups, but I see neither on this occasion. When an old Lakeland shepherd tells you it's 'gonna rain' though, you can't help but watch the sky all day, waiting for the cloud to build. (It never materialises; the oracle, on this day at least, is wrong.)

We're aiming for the old peat road that leads up on to Brantrake Moss. Like many Lakeland communities, Eskdale once relied heavily on peat as a major source of fuel. The material would be dug from areas such as Brantrake Moss and then dried and stored in huts, known as 'peat scales', on the moorland edge. Local families would then bring the peat down on sledges using carefully graded 'peat roads'. Several of these grassy tracks still exist today, zigzagging up the valley sides and providing easy routes for those with their sights set on the higher ground.

Back in 1983, Joss accessed the old peat road from the farm at Brant Rake, but there's no right of way here, so we carry on along the road in search of a little-used bridleway. Joss tells me the story of when his friend, Eddy, was driving in this area and knocked down a fox one evening. He picked it off the road, intending to bury it the next day, but when he got up in the morning, he discovered the fox wasn't dead at all; it'd come round. 'Car was a helluva mess,' laughs Joss.

As the River Esk brushes up against the road, he goes through the first gate he can find, clearly eager to head back on to the fells. 'The bridleway's a little further, Joss,' I say, but he goes his own way. I continue with Joss's friend, Pete 'Toddy' Todhunter, and we soon find a trail through the roadside trees and shrubs. At first, the bridleway skirts the base of Brantrake Crags. Above us are huge piles of shattered rock and dense bracken, combining to create almost impenetrable, potentially ankle-twisting ground. I've climbed peat roads before and I know they always find a way through or around such terrain, but it's hard to see how this one is going to manage it. Before long, we hear the sound of Joss's walking poles on the stony path behind us. Like those reliable peat roads, he's found a way through. 'Where you been, like?' Pete teases.

Resting near Devoke Water ▶

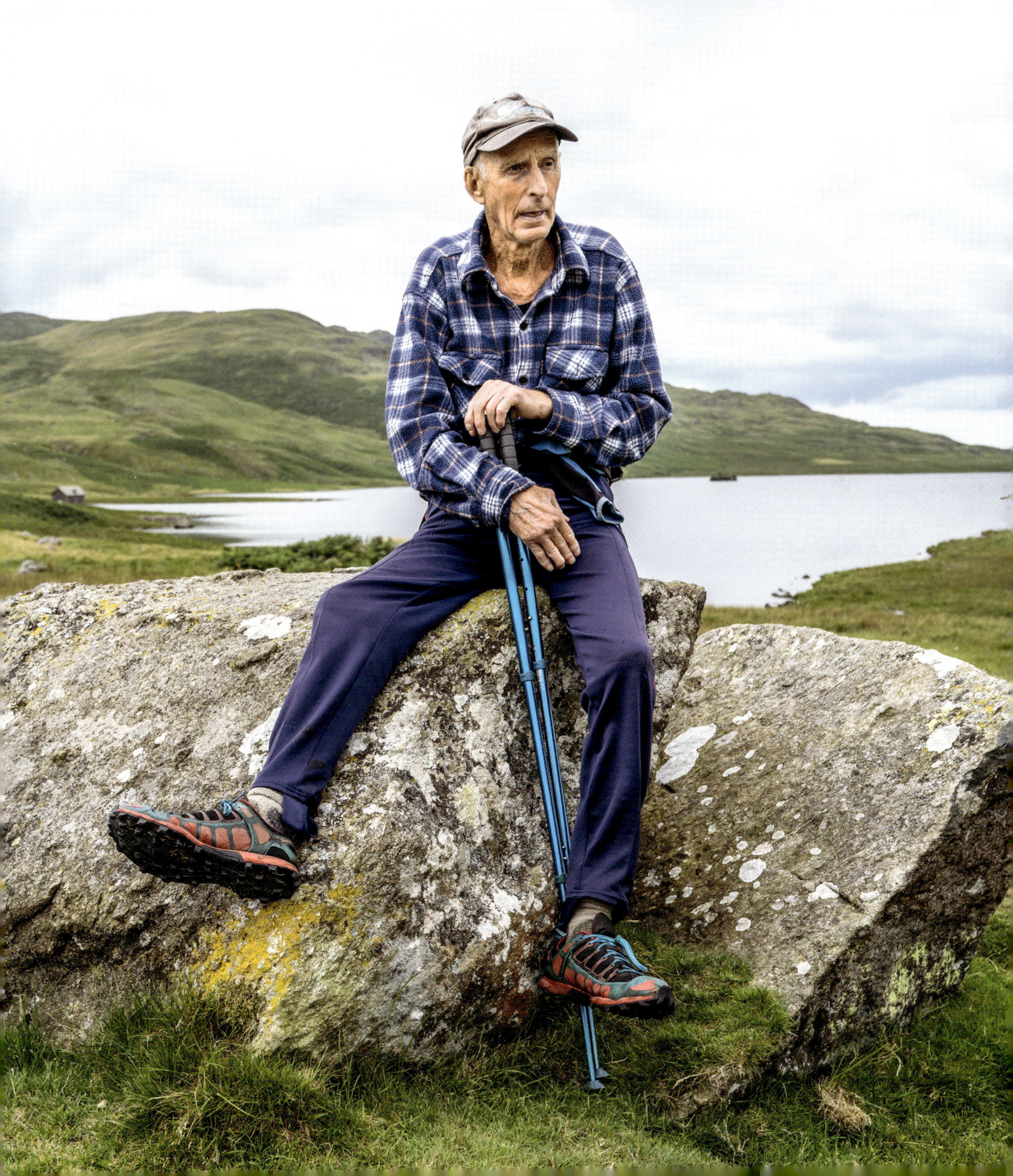

'Ahh, we stopped for coffee in 't la'al house down there,' he jokes.

As expected, the peat road finds a gap through the crags and begins climbing. Further up Eskdale, similarly ancient routes lead up to Blea Tarn, Low Birker Tarn, Kepple Crag and Brat's Moss. This one's less well walked, but its grassy ramps are still obvious, supported in places by low walls. 'It's nice and green,' says Joss, inspecting the way ahead. 'Those paths were well put in; they've stood the test of time.' It goes as far as the moss and then suddenly stops. This is where the peat-cutters would have worked. They didn't need to go any further. But for us modern walkers or runners wanting to get beyond this bleak area of flat, boggy ground, there's little to guide us now except for the occasional sheep trod. We can only trust that the sheep won't lead us into the soft heart of the bog.

These lonely, little-visited moors are dotted with the remains of ancient settlements

These lonely, little-visited moors are dotted with the remains of ancient settlements. The climate was considerably warmer and calmer in the early to mid Bronze Age – roughly 2500BC to about 1200BC – allowing people to move higher on to the fells. Many of Cumbria's prehistoric sites are located at about 500 to 1000ft above sea level. Barnscar, just over a mile south-west of Devoke Water, consists of substantial earthwork remains of both Bronze Age and Romano-British settlements, with enclosures, hut circles, field systems and cairns. Bronze Age pottery has been found here as well as an undated coin hoard, while aerial photographs have identified a stone avenue leading from Barnscar to Devoke Water.

It's hard to believe that ancient people once chose to live up here in what is now a rather forlorn landscape. Even in our modern society, where people crave solitude and are forever seeking out the quieter corners of our islands, relatively few make it to Devoke Water. As we stand beside the boathouse at the eastern end of the tarn, the only people we see are a woman with two young children. As the pair explore inquisitively, Joss chats easily with them, as he does with everyone. After they've gone, he remarks on how good it is to see children so happy, enjoying the outdoors and being encouraged to investigate their surroundings. He seems just as thrilled as they are, delighting in this place, this moment. He runs his hands along the boathouse's sturdy walls, explaining the techniques that went into building it. 'There's some bloody good cornerstones

Chapter 3 – Eskdale Green to Dunnerdale   47

▲ On the old peat road

▲ Boathouse at Devoke Water

here,' he says, rapping his knuckles against the structure. Posing for photographs, he crouches down to touch the tarn, laughing as his sunglasses fall into the water.

Back in 1983, Joss reached the water's edge at 09:11, still 29 minutes ahead of schedule. He wouldn't have visited the boathouse on that occasion though. 'I touched the water out there,' he says, indicating the north-eastern tip of Devoke Water 'and then went out on a line, just enough to clear the skyline'. Using one of his poles, he traces a route in the air, along the base of Seat How, the rocky lump that sits at the eastern end of the tarn overlooking the boathouse. 'The going would've been easier then, less vegetation, smoother grass, hardly any bracken. There would have been four or five times as many sheep as there are now.' The declining number of sheep on the fells is an issue he comes back to time and time again, something about which he feels strongly. 'Then I cut across to the road, just beyond where the farm track comes out.'

Unlike modern ultra-runners who plan their routes meticulously, often spending hours poring over digital mapping and spreadsheets before putting a foot on the ground, Joss took a simple approach. In the case of the LMW, he went out the weekend before and ran the route over two days. Even this would be unthinkable to today's runners...To run two consecutive days of about 50 miles

▲ The boathouse's sturdy walls have withstood the test of time

each, only a week before an attempt at a record. No way! They'd be taking it easy, tapering down, gathering energy for the big day.

Once on the ground, as Joss reached a high point, he would look ahead to work out where to go next. 'Just keep the vision of where you wanna go, and nine times out of ten that approach works out right,' he says.

'What about the tenth time?' I ask.

'You end up in a bloody bracken bed,' he says. Bracken and bog, it seems, are Joss's enemies on the fells.

The night before his big run, he made a special trip to reconnoitre the ground to the east of the Birker Fell Road. A friend had warned him of the bogs on that section, and he wanted to make sure he didn't end up stuck fast. 'I'd never seen any sheep or cattle on that patch, so I should've known it was wet ground,' he says. 'And those old peat holes that are grassed over can be dangerous. Some of them can be four or five feet deep. They're like basins, and because there's not many streams out there, they hold water. Once you're in the peat, it sucks you in. You've got to be wary of them areas. There's nowt worse than getting stuck in summat like that.'

Out on the Birker Fell Road, he points out the line he took 'along the lighter-coloured ground' where the sheep have been grazing. 'I kept to the right-hand side of the bog till I was past it and then cut under the crags to the wall. The ground back o' t' wall wasn't too bad; the sheep shelter there in bad weather, so they nibble at the grass. I thought it'd be faster, and it was. It was a good line. I ran back o' t' wall right to the fell-gate going into Wallowbarrow.'

The gate's gone now, but a replacement hurdle, while keeping sheep and cattle where they're meant to be, can be easily negotiated by walkers and runners. It provides access to one of the many long, narrow enclosures that lead from the open fell down into the valley. The rough ground is horribly wet as we wander around, trying to work out what Joss would've done in 1983. 'Was it this wet when you did it, Joss?' I ask as we rest on a rock outcrop, a welcome patch of dry ground.

'I was going that bloody fast, I didn't tek it in,' he says as he wrings out his socks.

'Did you have dry socks and fresh shoes at your rest stops?'

'I didn't have spare gear; couldn't afford it,' he replies, chuckling, before launching into a story about how he ran the 1971 Vaux Mountain Trial in a string vest and underpants. He won, despite his attire. 'I was wearing a string vest before Ron Hill was born! He took the bloody credit!' (He's referring to the 1938-born marathon runner and clothing entrepreneur who was famous, in the 1960s and 1970s, for running in a string vest.)

> 'I was wearing a string vest before Ron Hill was born!'

As the laughter dies down, we gaze out across Dunnerdale. Caw is streaked with silvery veins as the heavy rain of the previous two days continues to find a way off the fell. Looking downstream, towards where the Duddon empties into the Irish Sea, the sodden landscape sparkles in the sunshine, its beauty enhanced by the extra water.

Talk of the 1971 Mountain Trial has obviously brought back more memories for Joss, as he soon moves on to the 1975 event as well. 'That crag there on the skyline was the last checkpoint,' he says, indicating a rocky area on the other side of the valley. 'I was running really well coming in off Hardknott, and then I went in a bloody hole. I come out and I was bent double; I couldn't straighten up. And talk about sweat running off me!' Joss's two-day marathon partner Peter Walkington, of the Blackburn Harriers, then caught him up and, seeing he was struggling, wouldn't leave him. 'I went down past Levers Water, past the youth hostel and I was still running badly. Still Peter wouldn't leave us. I said, "Bugger off. You can win this easy." Anyways, he stopped with us. Then I said, "I'm going over t' tops because I'm not moving so fast". He's seen the checkpoint now and he's off like hell. I get to the last checkpoint and, as I swung me arse round to get me la'al ticket stamped, me back went in again. Peter was just disappearing over the side. So I went down t' green run, jumped t' wall, come right down the wet ground and I was sitting with me legs crossed at the finish when Peter stamped his card. I said, "What's kept you?" He must've looked back and thought, "Aye, that old bugger won't catch us!"' Joss won that event

▲ A bridleway leads from the Birker Fell Road to Devoke Water

– 19 miles (30.6km) and 8000ft (2439m) of ascent – in 4hr 37min 45sec, almost 10 minutes ahead of the second-placed Walkington.

We negotiate boulders and rock outcrops as we descend steeply, hemmed in by craggy ground up to our left and a wall to our right. 'It's a lovely way down,' Joss comments. The path, although little used by walkers, clearly has some vintage. It passes through woodland of birch, lime and the occasional oak before joining a bridleway beneath the imposing Wallowbarrow Crag. When we reach High Wallowbarrow, Joss stops to have a crack with the farmer, Chris

▲ In vest and underpants at the Mountain Trial, 1971
(Photo from Joss's own collection; photographer unknown)

▲ Negotiating rocky ground on the descent

▲ Joss chats with Chris Chinn and his son Ben, while sheepdog Brek gets some fuss

Chinn, about the lambing season just gone, about the National Trust, about old friends…Chris's son Ben is just getting into fell-running and Joss shares some words of wisdom, advising him to abandon his quad bike and get around the farm and the fells on foot as much as possible.

We push on, towards the River Duddon. Two herons are standing patiently beside some pools beneath the farm. 'They've got a lot of enemies, frogs and that,' says Joss. 'Those pools'll be a gold mine for 'em.' Large holes, ready to catch out the unwary, reveal the badgers have been busy. As attentive to detail as always, Joss points out an old stone drain emerging from a grassy slope and an enormous old sycamore, laden with the winged samara that will 'helicopter' the tree's seeds to the ground later in the year. Always the old-fashioned gentleman, he opens a gate and stands back for me to pass through. 'After you, young 'un.' He holds back some brambles that are encroaching on the path. 'Briars are taking over. The Trust should get on to this. A lot of people would be put off.'

The thundering Duddon is crossed on a narrow humpback bridge. Overhanging trees tickle the surface of the fast-moving river while, upstream, the crystal clear waters have to negotiate tremendous boulders that have tumbled down from Wallowbarrow Crag and now litter the channel. Here, deep pools of blue alternate with fast-moving rapids, and the sound of peregrines calling from the cliffs above is drowned out as one of Lakeland's most dramatic but least-known rivers gathers pace.

The Romantic poet William Wordsworth, who ranged far and wide across the Cumbrian landscape, fell in love with Dunnerdale when he was a schoolboy in Hawkshead in the 1780s. He returned many times as an adult, and even wrote a series of sonnets about his 'long-loved Duddon'. It remains a beautiful, largely unspoilt dale to this day. There's little here in the way of tourism infrastructure – a pub at Seathwaite, a simple farm campsite, one or two holiday cottages and B&Bs – and any visitors who do have the valley on their wish list will have a potentially tricky time reaching it. There's no public transport, and drivers approaching from the north will have to negotiate one of two tortuous roads, among the steepest in England – the Hardknott and Wrynose passes. In winter, when these are sheathed in ice or blocked by snow, the only way into the dale is via a long and winding road from Cumbria's remote south-western corner.

Despite it being a warm, dry day, there's no one about when we reach the valley road – no cars, no walkers, no farm traffic. The silence is broken only by the sound of Tarn Beck, seemingly the only thing that's in a hurry to get anywhere. Joss points out a bird on the church roof: a cormorant is watching us. Depending on where you are in the world, this could be taken as a sign of good luck or a bad omen. We're in Dunnerdale on a beautiful summer's day. It's clearly the former.

> It remains a beautiful, largely unspoilt dale to this day

JOHN'S STORY

John Wild was a world-class runner in the late 1970s and early 1980s, representing England in international cross-country and steeplechase events. Having turned his attention to fell-running, he was staying in the Lake District with his wife when word reached him of Joss's Lakes, Meres and Waters attempt. Would he like to join Joss? As a member of the Cumberland Fell Runners, John had already committed to taking part in the Blake Fell Race on the same day, but…why not?

'It was an early morning stint,' he recalls. 'My wife drove me to Ennerdale from where we were staying and we must've got there about six o'clock. I only planned to run with Joss to Wastwater – and my wife was there to pick me up – but I was enjoying it so much, I just kept going. You can't fail to enjoy the man's company – he's so knowledgeable and so likeable. I was thoroughly enjoying it.'

He remembers how, when Joss reached Ennerdale Water, Wastwater and Devoke Water, he crouched down to touch the water 'to prove he'd touched it; he hadn't just run past it'.

'On one occasion, we came upon a sheep on its back. Ewes, once they're on their backs, can't turn back over, and this poor beast had had its eyes pecked out too. So, Joss turned it over. He knew whose sheep it was, which is something that sticks in my mind. When we got down to the next feeding station, he told his wife whose sheep it was and which crag it was on so that she could contact the farmer.'

Instead of his planned 90-minute stint, John ran with Joss for two hours 40 minutes, staying with him as far as Devoke Water. He says he would've gone even further, but he didn't want to let his club down. Far from letting them down, he did them proud, not only competing in the Blake Fell Race later the same day but winning the 7-mile (11km) event in 47min 56sec.

Dunnerdale ▶▶

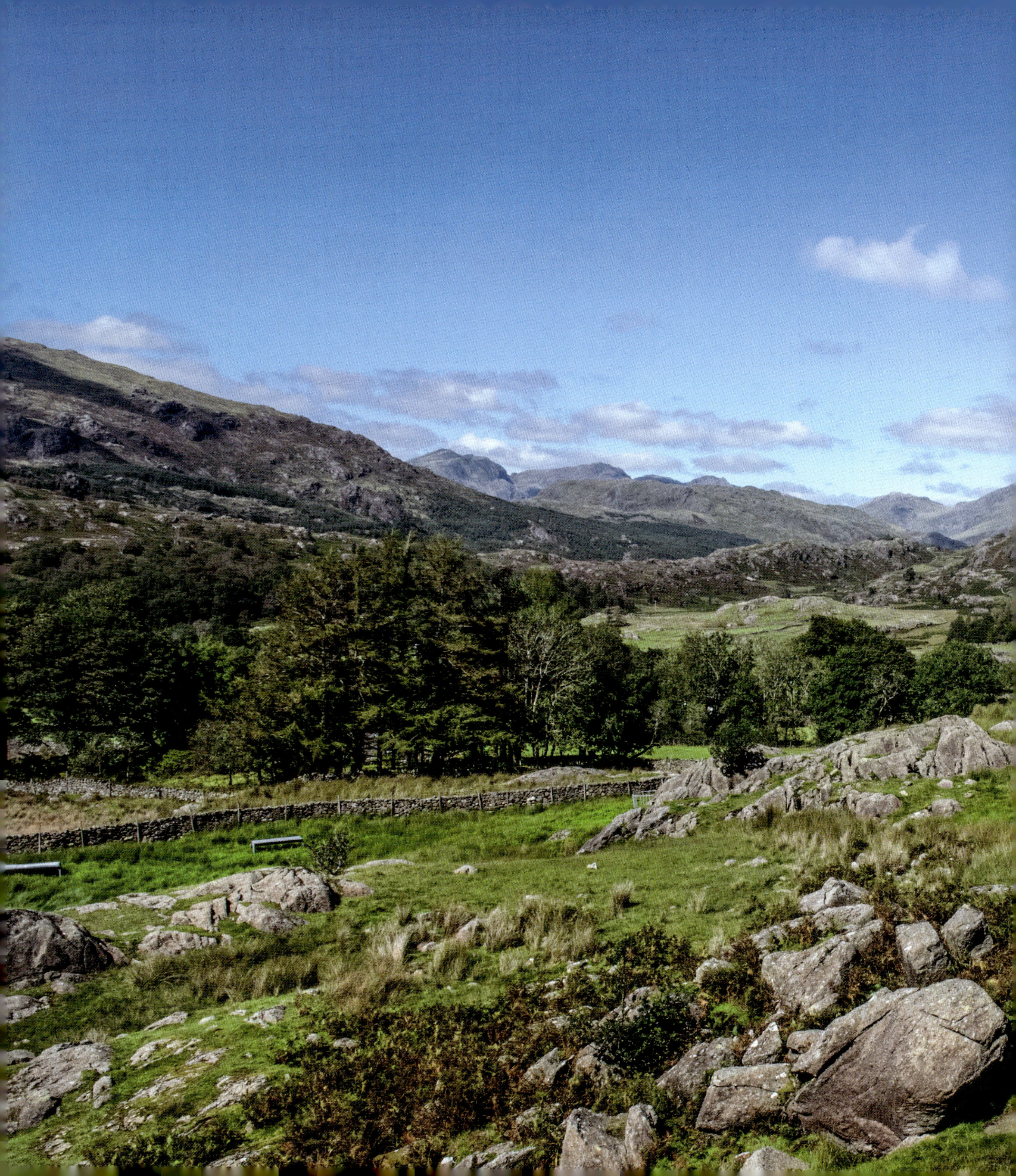

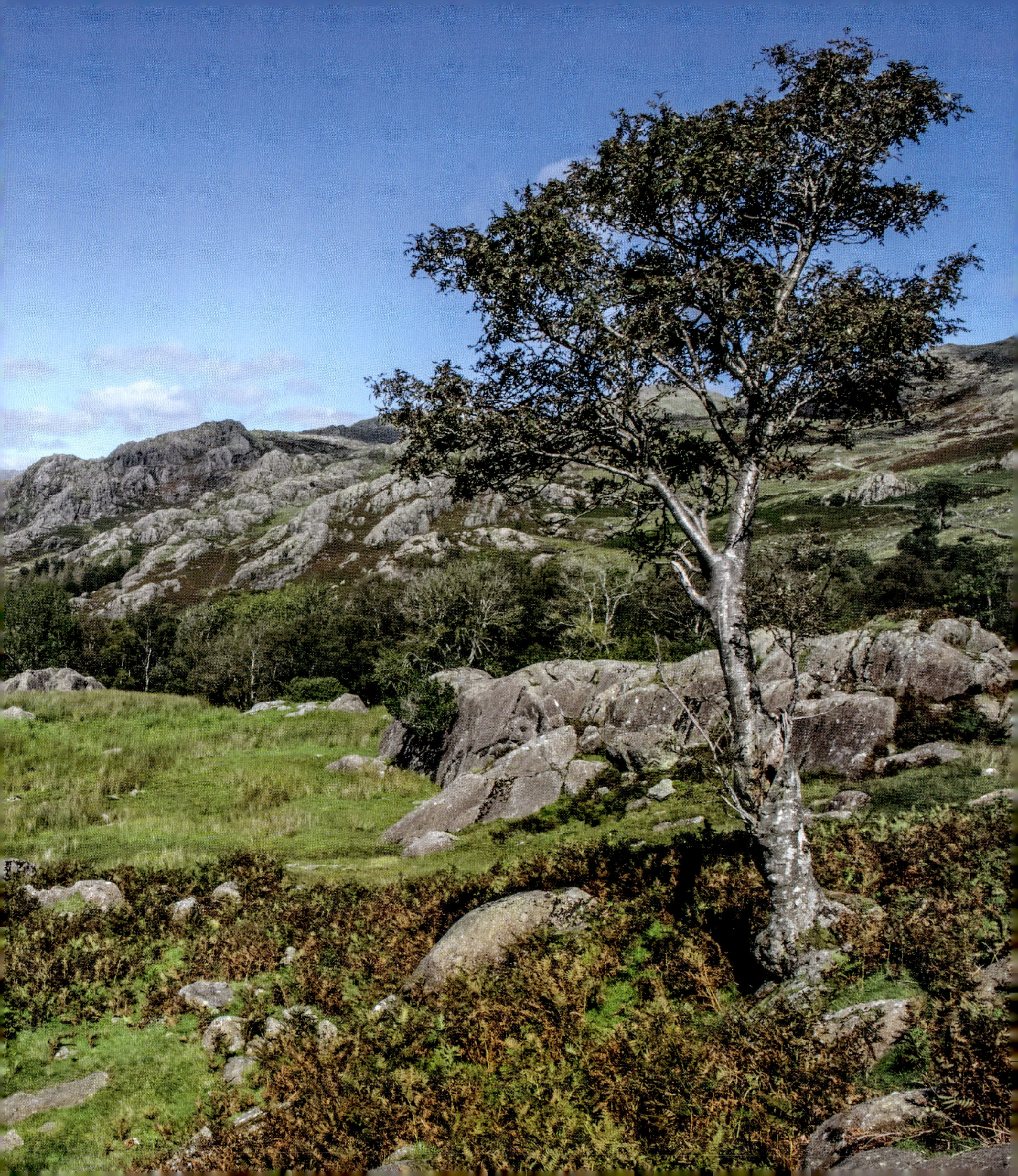

STAGE 3

Start Forestry England's Giggle Alley car park, Eskdale Green (NY 141 002)

Finish Holy Trinity Church, Seathwaite, Dunnerdale (SD 229 961)

Distance 9 miles (14.5km)

Ascent 1670ft (509m)

Approximate walking time 4hr 30min–5hr

- With your back to the parking area, turn left along the road. After 1.1 miles (1.8km), take the lane on the right – signed Birkby Road. Follow this for 575 metres and then join a bridleway signposted through the trees and bushes on the left. Beyond a small gate, follow the line of the wall north-east. After drawing level with the buildings below, stay on the old peat road as it begins zigzagging up the fellside.

- The route ahead becomes less obvious when it reaches the edge of Brantrake Moss. The best way to reach the eastern end of Devoke Water is to veer south-west at first, keeping to the drier ground west of the moss. Beyond Black Beck, head roughly south, keeping to the west of the rockier ground of **Water Crag**. As you cross its shoulder, swing east to drop on to a trod running parallel with the northern shore of **Devoke Water**. Descend rough ground to the tarn's eastern tip. A few strides beyond this, turn right along a vehicle track towards the boathouse. As the track bends right, near the water's edge, bear left along a rough, wet path parallel with the shore for 200 metres. Reaching Hall Beck, head south-east along a faint trail that becomes clearer as it nears the farm at **Woodend**. Enter the yard and then follow the access lane out to the road.

- Turn right along the road for 155 metres and then strike off east over pathless ground. The route climbs steadily over featureless, sometimes wet moorland and, after about 1 mile (1.6km), you'll encounter a wall. Follow this north-east for roughly 0.6 miles (1km) – until you reach a hurdle (former gate) in the wall at SD 20432 96880. Cross the hurdle and drop to the bottom, south-east corner of this long enclosure. Go through the gate and follow a fence line uphill (east). After a small gate in a wall, head east towards two large fence posts and then continue south-east, with a line of posts. Nearing a wall, bear east-south-east to follow the wall downhill. A trail slowly materialises. Turn right along the Wallowbarrow–Grassguards bridleway. At the

▲ Moody skies over the moorland near Devoke Water

farm at **High Wallowbarrow**, go left through the gate and follow the right of way east. On entering the woods, keep left at a fork. Cross the stone footbridge and climb beside the wall. After a gated bridge over **Tarn Beck**, keep close to the beck and, beyond a squeeze stile, you emerge on a road opposite Holy Trinity Church in **Seathwaite**.

Chapter 3 – Eskdale Green to Dunnerdale 57

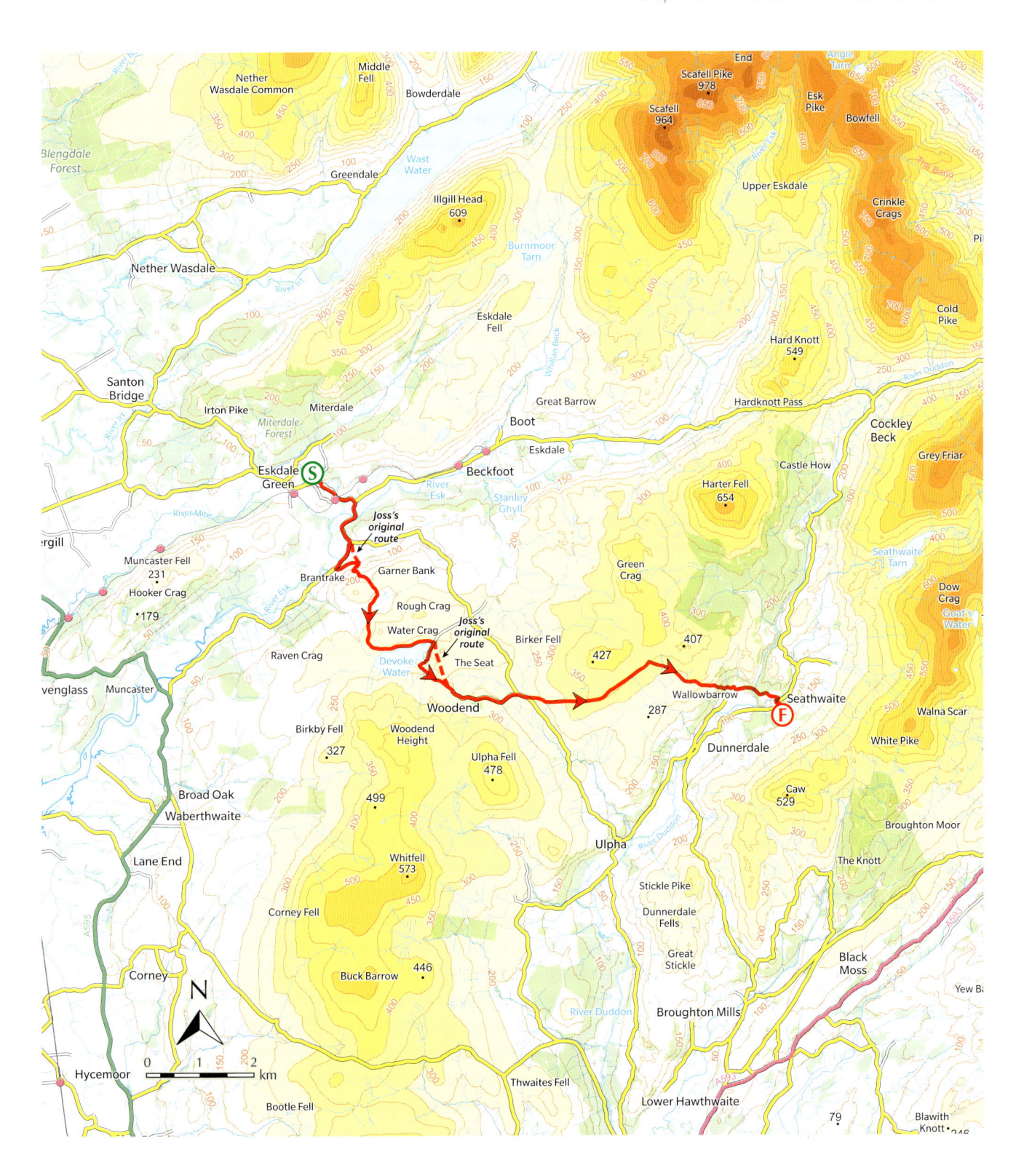

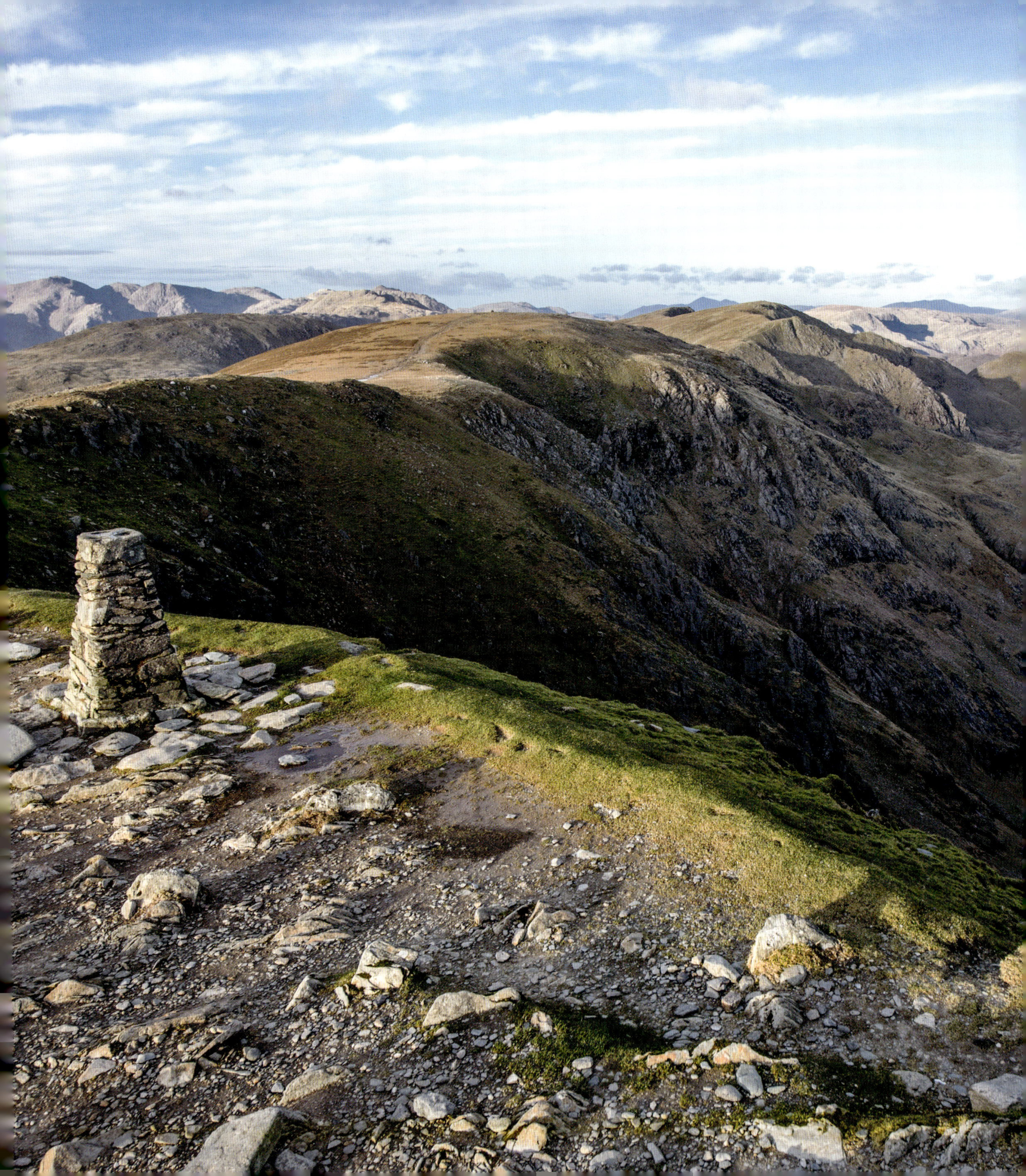

CHAPTER 4
Dunnerdale to Coniston
(Goat's Water, Low Water, Levers Water)

'It was absolutely beautiful as I come into the valley,' says Joss, recalling his 1983 run. 'The day had picked up.' He dropped on to the Dunnerdale road near Seathwaite's Newfield Inn, an area he'd not visited many times before. He was, however, very familiar with other parts of the valley from having run the Duddon Valley Fell Race on several occasions and from visiting his friend and fellow runner Ken Ledward, who lived at the bottom of the Walna Scar Road with his wife Liz.

'I ran a few of the early Duddon races when Ken used to put them on. He'd have the race on the Saturday, and an orienteering course on the Sunday.' This would've been in the late 1970s and early 1980s. 'The orienteering race would take you all over Dunnerdale and into the quarries. On the first one, Peter Nelson went off course. He ended up in this old quarry works and there were 15 or 20 people there, all wearing long coats. He said to me later, "They tried to make out they weren't there." I told him they'd be cock-fighting, and they'd have the birds hidden under their coats. That was the last time I heard of cock-fighting in the Lakes.'

Ken's name comes up a lot as we walk the Lake District, and it's clear that Joss has a lot of respect for his old friend. 'Him and Liz both did a lot for the sport. They put on the two-day Saunders Marathon as well. It was really well organised. There was even a beer wagon at night – a pint or two for the lads.'

Joss would think nothing of running from his Wasdale home to visit Ken and Liz for a cup of tea and a scone 'with plenty of jam on it'. 'If t' tops were clear, I'd run out back to Red Pike, from Bowderdale, over Pillar, back o' Kirk Fell, traverse Gable, up on till Esk Hause, and then across t' tops till Wrynose, up Wet Side Edge, run t' skyline into Seathwaite, have a cuppa with Ken and Liz, and then run back home.' Whenever he conjures up these favourite non-race runs, he has a tendency to stare into space, or close his eyes, as if he's transported back to an earlier time. He leaves the 21st century and the body of an 84-year-old man to glide, once again, over the fell tops with ease. I later plot his tea-and-scones route on the map and discover that what, for Joss, was just a day's outing would probably be a two-day backpack, even for reasonably fit hill-walkers – about 30 miles (48km) with 9000ft (2744m) of ascent.

◀ From the summit of the Old Man, with Levers Water (top) and Low Water visible to the right

▲ Richard Eastman with Juno
(Photo credit: Richard Eastman)

▲ No wasps today, hopefully

It's probably just as well there were no Ledwards (or cakes) in Dunnerdale to tempt Joss off course in 1983; instead, he simply pushed on with his running companion Richard Eastman. In 2020, as we climb the ladder stile just above the Rucksack Club's hut at High Moss, he suddenly remembers: 'There was a nest of wasps halfway down this stile. The dog was in front of us and he knocked it off.' He's talking about Richard's Dobermann, Juno, who accompanied them from Devoke Water to Goat's Water. 'A bloody great thing running on ahead all the time! You couldn't see path for dog; all you could see was its tail and its arsehole. It was a bloody nuisance.' Joss was stung by several of the wasps and was picking them out of his clothes for the next few miles. 'I lengthened me stride and went faster to get rid of the damn things, but they were stuck in me vest. Nasty things! One or two got the feeding of me.'

While a couple of young boulderers are unfolding their crash pads at the base of a small crag, we climb to the top of an ice-smoothed outcrop, crowned by a single tree. The air clarity is amazing. To the north, the magnificent Scafells seem close enough to touch, with the bulge of Broad Stand looming menacingly over Mickledore. It is the skyline to the east, though, that focuses our

> **To the north, the magnificent Scafells seem close enough to touch**

attention – the Coniston Fells. They might lack substance from this angle, but their true nature will soon be revealed...

'So what's the Walna Scar like to run, Joss?' I ask, referring to the old track that links Dunnerdale and Coniston, crossing a high pass along the way. I expect him to be disparaging, condemning the loose, stony surface that so many runners and walkers, myself included, detest, but he's as positive as ever.

'It's nice, aye. We had a great run up there; me legs were good for climbing. We cut corners on 't other side, the zigzags. I dropped in just below Blind Tarn and then I had a real good line right through till Goat's Water. I've been to Blind Tarn a lot of times, doing different events – Mountain Trials, two-day marathons, all sorts. It's a secluded place, not very well travelled; there's steep ground all around it except where it comes out.'

Joss followed the most direct line possible, one that saw him traversing some rough ground, scrambling over or running round a series of rock outcrops. Goat's Water would've put in an appearance only as he passed beneath Blind Tarn Screes. The Achille Ratti Climbing Club, which now coordinates the '26 Lake, Meres and Waters' challenge run, recommends a slightly lower line, leaving the Walna Scar Road just below Goatfoot Crags. Alternatively,

The Old Man towers over Goat's Water ▶

there's a good path just below Torver Bridge that leads all the way to Goat's Water. Whichever route is taken, there's a real sense now of re-entering serious fell country – for the first time since Haycock and the ground above Greendale. To the west, aprons of grey scree and imposing buttresses lead up to the summit of Dow Crag while, to the east, the rugged slopes of the Old Man are punctured by disused quarry workings. Between them, comfortable in its glacial bowl, sits Goat's Water, the seventh body of water into which Joss dipped his fingers.

'Past Blind Tarn, I just got on to a bit of decent running that takes you on the contour till Goat's Water. It was good. There was a heron standing on one leg fishing when I got there, and two BNFL lads. They were supposed to run over t' top of Old Man with me but they didn't look like they had a lot in their legs so I contoured round with them. It worked though. I come out at a good spot – only mebbe 50 metres from Low Water.' The two BNFL lads to whom Joss refers would have been apprentices from the Sellafield nuclear site (owned at the time by British Nuclear Fuels Ltd), where Joss worked as a storeman.

Retracing Joss's contouring route in 2020 proves easier said than done – crags, boulders, scree and the vertiginous edge of a sheer-sided quarry pit confirm this is not the line he took in 1983.

'We climbed out too early,' he later confirms. It takes longer than anticipated, but the tourist path from Coniston village to the Old Man is eventually reached, and there, just below, is Low Water. 'It's a magic place, you know, is Low Water,' says Joss.

> There's a real sense now of re-entering serious fell country

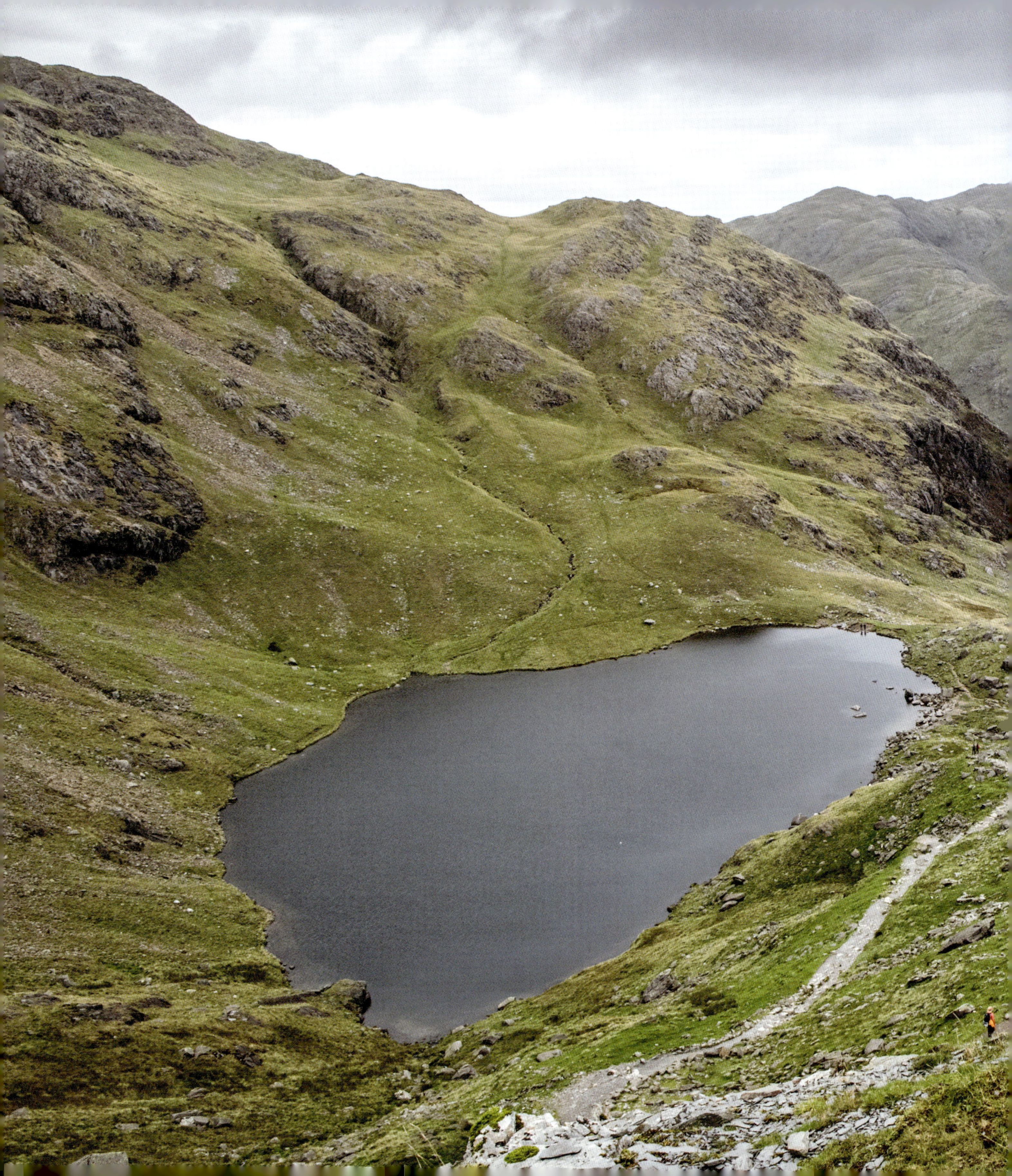

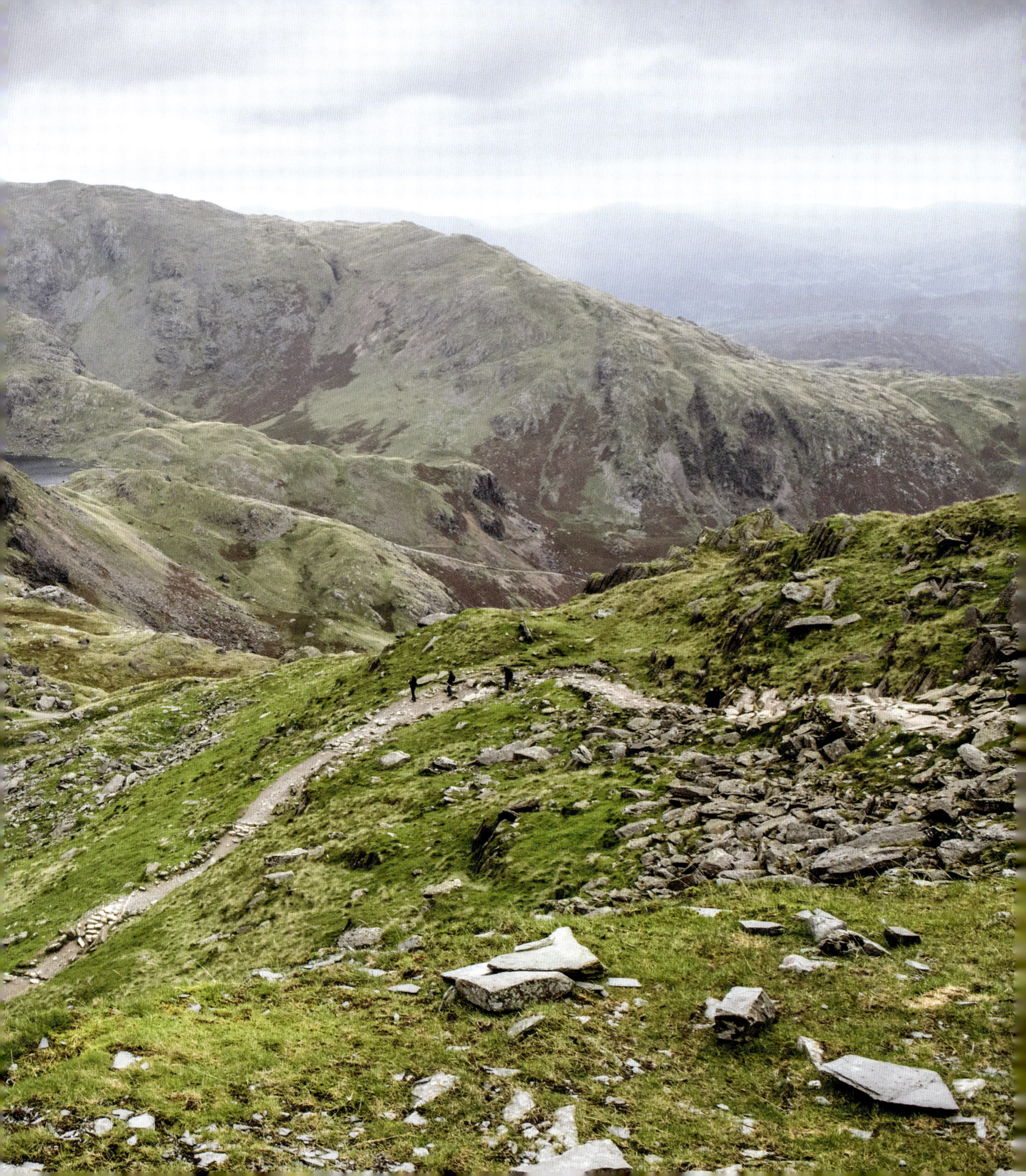

'Especially when the sun's in the right place. It's in, like, this slate cocoon, and there's different colours of rock. When there's high cloud floating about and you have time to be at the right place to look in, it's really summat special. It was a bit like that on that morning, but I didn't have much time to stand.'

Even though he was now 39 minutes ahead of schedule, there was no hanging around. It took him just nine minutes to cover the ground between Low Water and Levers Water, against an anticipated 30 minutes, now putting him a whole hour up on his own ambitious projection. He used a grassy rake that occupies a safe ledge slanting down Brim Fell's eastern crags. Once well grazed, the line was obvious in 1983, but it's less so now. There's not much here to confirm you're in the right place and not heading for a cliff edge. A pair of rusty rails protrudes from a damp fellside hole fringed by heather and ferns. Beyond the mine opening, the rails disappear round a bend, into the dripping darkness. Joss has no recollection of seeing this adit in 1983 but, travelling at more than four miles per hour over such tricky terrain, that's hardly surprising. He does, however, remember a sheep running on ahead of him. 'There was an old yow with a lamb, and they'd seen us coming. It looked at us and went straight through on that same line, all the way till Levers Water. That's what it must've done when it was gathered. It knew what it was up to.'

Like Goat's Water and Low Water before it, Levers Water started life as a natural corrie tarn, occupying a crag-girt hollow scooped out by a glacier thousands of years ago. Meltwater would have been trapped behind the deposit of rocks and other debris left by the retreating ice. In the case of Levers Water, that natural dam has been enhanced in more modern times by an artificial, stone-built barrier. This had the effect of enlarging the tarn and controlling its outflow so that its water could be used to power the nearby mine workings.

> 'It's a magic place, you know, is Low Water'

◄◄ Looking down on Low Water

▲ Covering ground on the Coniston Fells

▲ Levers Water started life as a natural tarn

Despite human interference, it remains a magnificent spot, and, if you can ignore the small dam, it's easy to believe it's entirely natural. 'It's a bigger water than you're aware of, in't it?' suggests Joss. To the west, dark shadows give the impression that the crags project out over the screes and water below, defying gravity; to the north, the sunlight reveals the true angle of the cliffs, steep but not overhanging. 'There's a goose bield under those crags there,' he says. 'There's only two in the Lake District; the other one's on Great Borne. It's wide in the bottom and gradually...' He demonstrates, with his hands, how the small dry-stone construction tapers, and explains how it would've been baited, possibly with a goose, to entice a fox. Once inside, the animal would've been trapped, unable to climb the corbelled walls.

It's hard to turn your back on such scenery, but the village of Coniston beckons as the route heads away from the hills to begin a long section through lowland woods and valleys. It's impossible now to turn a blind eye to the area's industrial heritage. Just south of Levers Water, before the descent even begins, are some fences that prevent walkers – and sheep – from wandering into the frighteningly deep holes known as the Back Strings. These form part of the original Coniston copper mines worked by German miners in the early 17th century. The Germans, at that time the best miners in Europe, were first invited to England by Elizabeth I in 1564. She was in desperate need of their skills. With the Spanish knocking at the door, Good Queen Bess wanted copper to make cannons and for the minting of coins. Nobody in Europe at the time could locate the ore, extract it and then smelt it like the Germans could. They were the men for the job. Employed by the Company of Mines Royal, they established copper and lead mines throughout Cumbria, their centre of operations being Keswick. In the Coniston Fells, they drove tunnels 200ft deep, but by the middle of the 19th century, men were working up to 1100ft beneath the surface.

It's hardly surprising that sinister legends grew up around these dark holes in the ground, into which men would disappear and not always re-emerge. The prominent cleft in the rock on the other side of Levers Waterfall is Simon's Nick, named after a local man who is said to have sold his soul to the devil in return for riches in copper. The result? He died in one of the first mining accidents involving gunpowder.

From the descending track, we look down on the remains of some of the operations associated with the Industrial Revolution, including the Paddy End dressing floors. Carts, tramways and horses would have brought the ore down to this area so that workers, including children, could sort and dress it ready for transportation. Further on still, the Bonsor smelt mill and the old mine office, now a YHA hostel, are passed.

Joss remembers running this section at a fair lick. 'That lad I was with didn't half leg it down that bloody path there – and it's a fair way from Levers Water till the top of Coniston Water. He was going at racing speed, not a steady pace, like. I was okay though; I just sat on his shoulder. But it would've been a stride too fast if he'd been going on for another section.'

It wasn't speed though that caused Joss to go wrong as they entered the village. 'There were that many people and cars as we were coming into Coniston, everything was gridlocked. It was manic. I'd been through there before and knew where I was going, but I must've gone wrong somewhere. I wasn't concentrating and I was just trying to get on, but there were that many folk, I couldn't get my mind round it. I ended up in a cul-de-sac.' He was already considerably ahead of schedule though, so this minor setback didn't dent his time. He finally reached the shores of Coniston Water at 11:43, still 47 minutes up on estimates. Enough time for a little treat...

> **Sinister legends grew up around these dark holes in the ground**

CUMBRIA'S MINING HERITAGE

Humans have been chipping away at the Cumbrian fells for millennia. The earliest known mines are high above Mickleden, where Neolithic people roughed out axe heads from a seam of greenstone in the Langdale Pikes. One such 'axe factory' is on Pike o' Stickle's steep, scree-covered slopes. It's practically inaccessible today, but, several thousand years ago, as well as quarrying the exposed rock, Stone Age people were working their way into the fell via a short tunnel – mining, in fact.

Historians suspect that lead ore was being extracted in the North Pennines in Roman times – in the Alston area, close to Cumbria's modern borders with Northumberland and County Durham. The invaders used the metal in their aqueducts, to create pewter and for guttering in their villas. They were also quite fond of that rather nice, shiny element often found encased in the lead ore: silver. The Romans were probably busy exploiting other riches among the Cumbrian hills – Britain's mineral wealth was, after all, one of the key reasons they set their sights on our little island in the first place – but evidence of their activities is hard to find, particularly where it's been chipped, blasted and generally hacked at by subsequent operations.

The scars left by mining and quarrying that we see on the fells today have almost all been created since Elizabethan times. The Industrial Revolution, in particular, brought a massive surge in demand for just about every mineral then known to mankind, and Cumbria was home to some of the biggest and busiest operations in the British Empire.

▲ Runner Iain Irving joins Joss in Coniston Water (Photo credit: Dave Elliott)

IAIN'S STORY

Iain Irving got to know Joss through the Sellafield apprentice training centre. He wasn't a fell-runner but, as a member of the Workington Zebras rugby union 'Colts' team, he did a lot of distance running to improve his general fitness and signed up to join Joss on the stretch from Goat's Water to Coniston Water. He remembers setting off from Torver early in the morning and walking to Goat's Water.

'This was the first time I'd visited Goat's Water and I was taken aback by the clarity and turquoise colour of the small lake. When we saw Joss approaching, I got a huge lump in my stomach. We knew him not only as a storeman at Sellafield who would dispense "long stands", "spirit-level bubbles" and "tartan paint" without the correct paperwork, but also as a world-class sportsman, something that inspired many of us apprentices.

'He looked perfectly fresh as he approached. A couple of quick "hellos" later and we were off. The first climb was reasonably hard going but I found the pace, if not comfortable, certainly achievable without too much pain, so I was in a very confident frame of mind, thinking this fell-running lark isn't that hard after all. Suddenly, Joss disappeared, and I quickly came to realise the best way to make time is to use your energy to the best effect – a good life lesson! I kicked on, managed to make up ground and we carried on comfortably until Low Water.' From here, things became wetter underfoot...

'As Joss flew, almost literally, down the fellside, deftly bounding from one solid area to another, I hit every water-filled, foul-smelling hole on that particular piste, which is why there's a photo of me cleaning off in Coniston Water later. We eventually got to the road and I was feeling the pain; Joss, unsurprisingly, seemed absolutely fine and even tried speaking to me. I think I managed a grunt.'

STAGE 4

Start Holy Trinity Church, Seathwaite, Dunnerdale (SD 229 961)

Finish North-west shore of Coniston Water at end of Lake Road, Coniston (SD 308 970)

Distance 9.9 miles (15.9km)

Ascent 3590ft (1095m)

Approximate walking time 6–7hr

▲ Joss makes canine friends

▶ Head north-east along the minor road for 0.25 miles (400 metres) and turn right along the access track to **Turner Hall Farm**. As the lane bends right, bear left through a large gate. Turn left at a track junction and go through a gate. Pass to the left of the cottages at High Moss. After the next gate, climb the ladder stile up to the right and then make your way roughly north-east across damp, pathless ground. At a surfaced lane, turn right. When the way ahead splits, keep right – along the **Walna Scar Road**.

▶ Follow this clear track for 2.4 miles (3.9km), crossing a high pass along the way. Take the path on the left 320 metres beyond the bridge over **Torver Beck**. This climbs to **Goat's Water** and then continues, more steeply, to **Goat's Hawse**. Turn right in the col and keep right at any forks.

▶ From the summit furniture on top of the **Old Man**, follow the well-walked path down the fell's north-east face. After **Low Water**, continue downhill for a further 0.6 miles (1km) and then turn left. Beyond the distinctive Pudding Stone, continue on the path up through Boulder Valley. At the top of the rise, drop to **Levers Water** and make your way along its southern shore. Cross the dam. (If the water level is too high, you'll have to complete a clockwise circuit of the reservoir to reach the eastern side of the dam.)

▶ Take the broad track following **Levers Water Beck** downstream. This performs several sharp bends as it descends, always staying on the eastern side of the beck. At a junction with a vehicle track, turn left, and follow this past the YHA's Coniston Coppermines hostel. Leaving the mine workings behind, watch for the gated Miners Bridge on your right. Cross this and turn sharp left. When this path emerges on a lane next to the Sun pub on the edge of **Coniston** village, turn right and then left at the T-junction. Go straight over the **A593** and follow Lake Road all the way to **Coniston Water**.

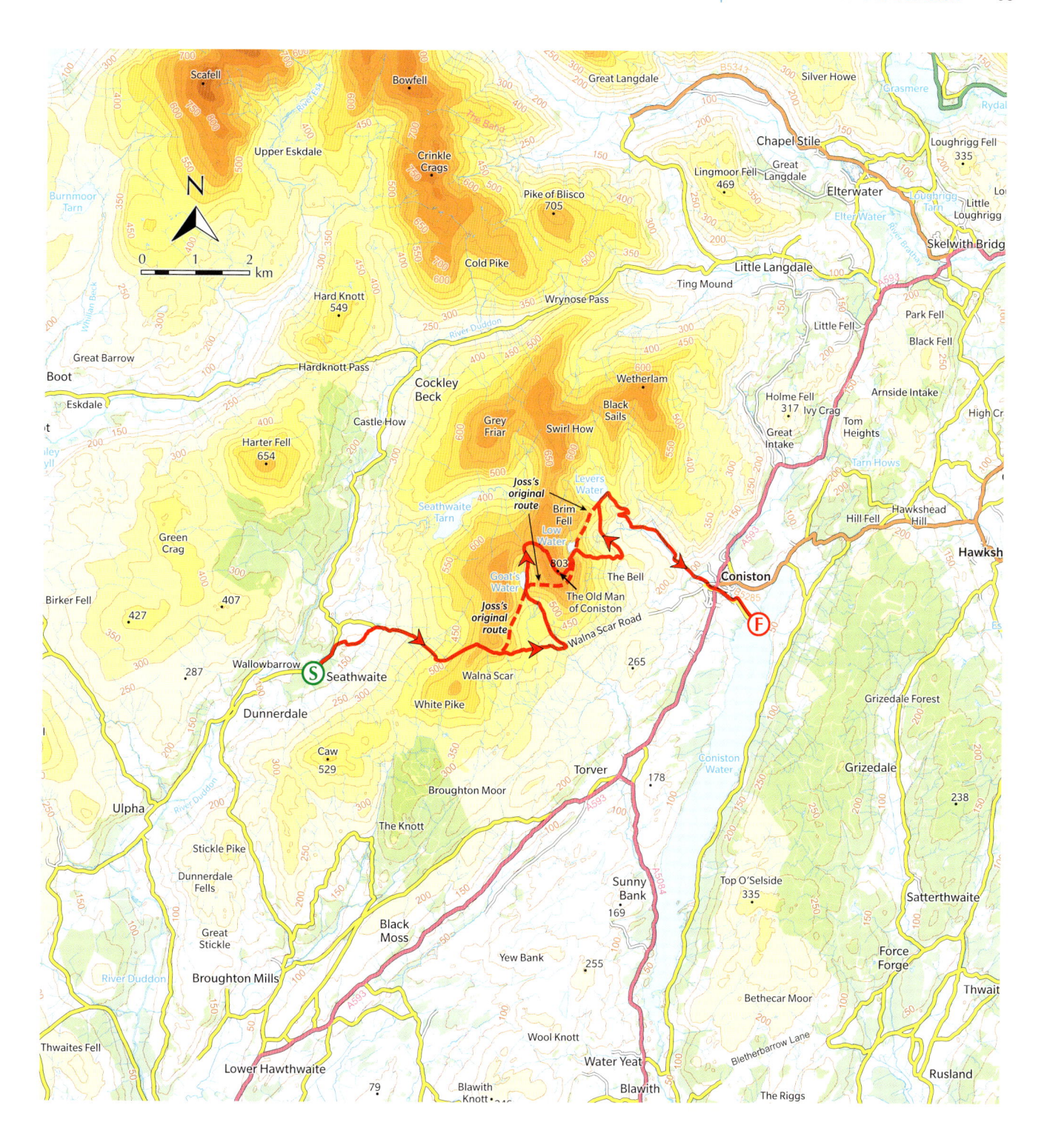

Chapter 4 – Dunnerdale to Coniston 69

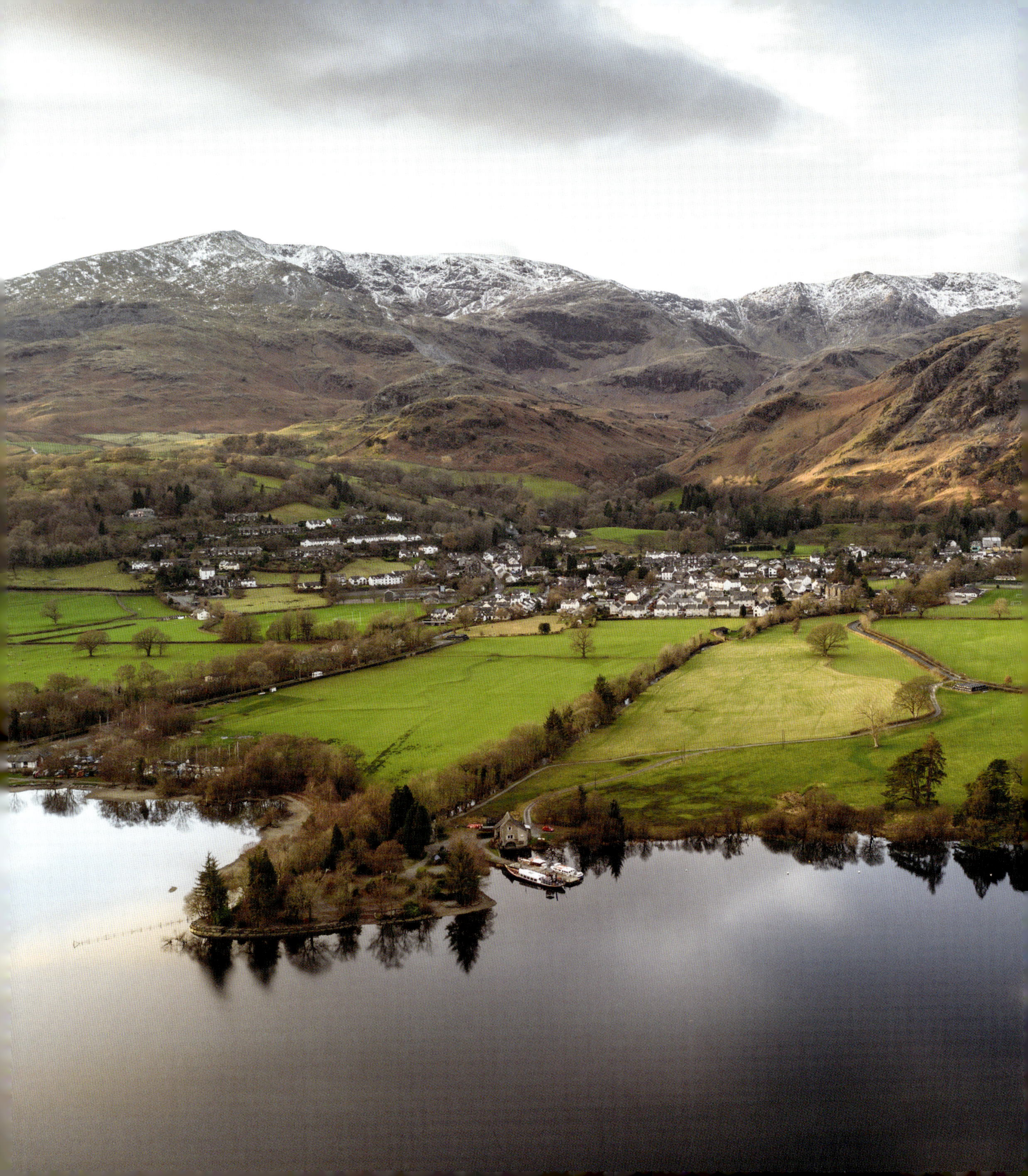

CHAPTER 5
Coniston to Skelwith Bridge
(Coniston Water, Esthwaite Water)

After hours of running on the fells with just his pacemakers for company, Joss found the summer crowds of Coniston disorientating. Even the usually busy honeypot of Buttermere had been silent as he'd passed by in the early hours of the morning. In the six hours since then though, while he'd been scaling high tops, dodging bogs, outrunning wasps and negotiating rough, remote terrain, the holidaymakers had eased their way into their lazy day, eating leisurely breakfast fry-ups and leaving their hotels and their B&Bs to start a day of gentle sightseeing. By the time Joss reached the shores of Coniston Water, it was almost midday and there were big crowds milling around, enjoying the June heat and the Lakeland scenery.

'It was a day for eating ice creams'

Behind them, the village of Coniston, with its tiered rows of miners' and quarrymen's cottages, squatted at the foot of the rugged mountains; to the south, the slender ribbon of Coniston Water, never more than about half a mile wide, reached out five miles into the distance, edging ever closer to the estuaries and shifting sands of Morecambe Bay. This is the lake where Malcolm Campbell and his son Donald broke one water speed record after another in the 20th century, the latter coming to grief in January 1967 while attempting to smash through the 300-mile-per-hour barrier in his jet-powered hydroplane *Bluebird K7*. It's also the lake that is home to Peel Island, said to be the inspiration for the fictional Wild Cat Island where John, Susan, Titty and Roger set up camp in Arthur Ransome's *Swallows and Amazons* children's adventure story.

Joss and Iain, with the support crew now alongside, stood out among the tourists. 'Everyone was sitting down by the lakeside; it was a day for eating ice creams,' Joss recalls. 'We were trying to run between all the people and they were looking at us as if we were silly buggers. But they do, don't they? You come down from the fell, sweat running down your legs...'

The holiday atmosphere was contagious though, and even Joss succumbed, joining the team in a moment of ice-cream indulgence. Joss's diet has long been a thing of legend among other fell-runners; he's a man who can go for hours without eating a thing,

◀ The village of Coniston, its lake and its fells

▲ The northern end of Coniston Water

making do with an occasional mouthful of water from mountain becks. When he was competing in his first races in the 1960s, sports drinks, as such, hadn't been invented – Lucozade, generally sold only in pharmacies in its orange, crinkly cellophane wrapper, was marketed as a pick-me-up to aid recovery after illness – and gels were still a long way off.

'I didn't eat a lot that day,' he says, recalling his 1983 run. 'I just nibbled here and there – one of them Mars bars or just a bit of a sandwich. And there was that one ice cream, of course. I'd tek in more liquid than owt else. I used to go all day, sometimes 10 hours of shepherding, on nowt – just a drink of water out of a stream. You

> Joss's diet has long been a thing of legend among other fell-runners

didn't think about hunger. On the Ennerdale Race, I used to keep a bottle up on Hay Stacks, hidden in a la'al bit of heather – always in the same spot. It'd have some juice in it, mebbe blackcurrant, with one of those salt tablets and mebbe three heaped tablespoons of glucose. It'd be enough to keep the cramp away.'

From Coniston Water, the route heads towards Hawkshead where Esthwaite Water awaits. Today, a series of roadside trails keeps cyclists and walkers away from the traffic as far as Monk Coniston, but Joss says they didn't exist in 1983; for much of the next 10 miles or so, he ran on the roads. 'It must've been a bit dull, after being on the fells?' I suggest.

On the contrary. 'I was switched off, floating along,' Joss tells me. 'The sun was shining and I was under no pressure. It was all good.'

Looking at it in retrospect, he realises this was an opportunity to see parts of the Lake District he'd never seen before. Joss is a fellsman. He'd been shepherding from a young age, gathering sheep from the high ground most of his life. So, to run through these idyllic central valleys and cross lower fells was a rare treat for him.

The route skirts the edge of the sprawling Grizedale Forest, passes the pretty, white-washed Baptist chapel at Hawkshead Hill, where worshippers have been meeting since 1709, and then heads out over farmland. From here, the views open out again. Less than two miles to the north-east, a surprisingly lofty obelisk stands proud on the humble little summit of Latterbarrow. Beyond the rolling, green pastures and the stone-walled enclosures, the high fells again beckon – the Fairfield group and Red Screes among them. The Kentmere fells are visible too – the next area of high ground on the LMW, still almost 20 miles away.

Whether you're attracted to the mountains or the dales, it's hard not to be moved by the scene and to feel drawn to explore more of it.

We drop into Hawkshead via Vicarage Lane, the past always crowding the present as we make our way through the historic village's maze of narrow alleyways. These lanes are just wide enough to allow a horse and cart to pass through, essential given Hawkshead's role in the past as a centre for the wool trade. In places, the buildings feature jetties where the upper storey projects out over these passageways, providing more internal space for the residents. Down a lane to our left is the 16th-century cottage where a young William Wordsworth lodged with Ann Tyson while attending the local grammar school. Having lost his mother a few years earlier, he is said to have adored the kind and maternal Mrs Tyson.

Joss recalls his first impressions of the village: 'Coming into it on a fine, sunny afternoon, everything looked fresh and beautiful...A lovely little place. And the church on the hill! The person

> We drop into Hawkshead via Vicarage Lane, the past always crowding the present

▲ St Michael and All Angels, Hawkshead

▲ Esthwaite Water is one of the lesser-known lakes

who put that up there had tremendous foresight. They should've been very proud of that. It'll be up there forever.' He's referring to the picturesque church of St Michael and All Angels, built on the site of an earlier chapel in about 1300.

Revisiting Hawkshead in 2020, Joss admits to feeling a slight sense of disappointment. The church, of course, is still there, as are the quaint cottages and cobbled lanes, but a plethora of pubs, cafés and other businesses shatters his memories of an unspoilt Lakeland settlement. 'There's been a fair bit of development,' he says, looking around. 'It's altered; it's more commercial. A few more properties have gone up, and it's lost its originality. You don't expect a place to stand still, but that day I came through in 1983, it felt like summat special. I think I had a vision that it would be just like it was on that day.'

The next lake, Esthwaite Water, doesn't disappoint though. Just south of the village, this relatively shallow, reed-fringed body of water is about one-and-a-half miles long and just a few hundred yards wide. It's one of the lesser-known lakes and, although lacking the grand, fell surroundings of most of the others, it has a tranquillity that brings with it a quality unmatched elsewhere in the National Park. In the poem 'Expostulation and Reply', Wordsworth reflects on a half-day spent sitting beside the water on an 'old grey stone' in a state of 'wise passiveness'. As he suggests, it seems to be the sort of place that encourages the visitor to 'dream your time away'.

'It's summat out of this world. You just don't expect to see a lake there'

'I wouldn't have known that Esthwaite Water existed if I hadn't done the Lakes, Meres and Waters,' Joss admits. 'It's summat out of this world. You just don't expect to see a lake there. It's hardly in the Lake District, is it? You can't help but wonder, "What am I doing down here?" But it's got be done. It's an area I'd never have gone if it wasn't for that day, but I'm pleased I did.'

The lake is privately owned and there's little public access to the shore. Those wanting to complete a lake circuit on foot have to take to the roads some way back from the water's edge, while those wanting to break the surface, as Joss did in 1983, have few opportunities. A minor road passes close to the water's edge at its southern end but the only access to the northern shore is via Waterside House, from where an almost invisible, often soggy right of way leads down as far as The Nab. 'When we were going out till Esthwaite Water back then, we were accosted by these two people who didn't have anything better to do, wanting a fight as we

▲ Alan Jackman (left) and Alastair Young with Joss at Esthwaite Water (Photo credit: Dave Elliott)

went past Waterside.' They told him he couldn't access the shore, and wanted him to turn back. 'They got a bit aggressive, but they didn't interview us for long; I told them I wasn't putting up with their nonsense. You have to be firm with those people. They wouldn't be allowed to block a right of way, not legally.'

I suggest they wouldn't have stood a chance of catching the fleet-of-foot Joss even if they'd wanted to. 'Not in them days,' he says wistfully.

Today, there's hardly anyone around – just a couple of fishermen out on the water in a rowing boat. The lake is home to one of the largest trout fisheries in north-west England and, with ecological improvements in recent years, is steadily returning to a more natural state. A new process has been introduced by water company United Utilities to reduce the amount of phosphates in any treated water entering the lake; a pipeline has been constructed to cut the amount of stormwater overflowing into it during heavy rain; and the fishery has moved from stocking rainbow trout to native brown trout. It's all looking very encouraging for the wild salmon that used to migrate through Esthwaite Water to their natural spawning grounds in the headwaters above, and ospreys have clearly already given it the thumbs-up, returning to the area after a very long absence.

Ospreys have clearly already given Esthwaite Water the thumbs up

Close to the shores of the far end of the lake is Near Sawrey, the village where Beatrix Potter once lived. Having spent a family holiday near Esthwaite Water in 1896, she fell in love with the area, and even used the lake as a setting for one of her most popular books, *The Tale of Mr Jeremy Fisher*. In Lakeland terms though, her books are just a small part of her legacy; more important is the land that she snapped up to protect it from development. On her death in 1943, all of this property, and the farms and cottages on it, was bequeathed to the National Trust to be protected in perpetuity for the benefit of the nation – a massive 4000 acres (1600 hectares) in total. Joss entered Potter country as soon as he reached the Coniston area, and for several hours continued to pass farms and land once owned by the children's author. As we walk back through Hawkshead on our way north to Skelwith Bridge, we pass the former offices of Potter's solicitor husband, William Heelis, now home to the Beatrix Potter Gallery run by the National Trust.

▲ Joss would rather be on the fells than in the valleys

As a farmer himself, Joss has mixed feelings about the Trust. Although he appreciates the work the conservation charity has done in some parts of the Lake District, he's very scornful of its approach to farming. 'It's sad really what the Trust has done. Them little farms of Beatrix Potter's – some are just growing bracken these days.' He swipes, with one of his walking poles, at the fronds of the ubiquitous green menace growing beside the path, a plant that has been steadily increasing its stranglehold on the fellsides as livestock numbers have been reduced. 'Those farms could've been a living for someone who wanted to be a farmer. And those people could've learnt how to put walls up and look after the environment. But the Trust don't want locals, and they want the sheep off the fells.'

Joss farmed at Bowderdale in Wasdale for many years ▶

National Trust

Bowderdale Farm

▲ Joss feels the National Trust has mismanaged his home valley, Wasdale

He also feels that the way the charity has managed his home valley, Wasdale, has been misguided at best. 'Wasdale Head should've been looked after. In my eyes, it's the jewel of England. Why the hell did they let it get in such a state? They've tekken sheep off t' fells, they want to plant trees that are useless…Everything used to be in good nick – it was all farmed.' He says the Trust has also failed to handle the valley's soaring visitor numbers adequately, always responding too late to problems such as eroded footpaths, litter, residents' driveways being blocked by parked cars, and tourists defecating in the churchyard of St Olaf's.

He goes quiet for a moment, ruminating on the damage he believes has been wrought on Wasdale, and then suddenly perks up with a memory of one tiny personal victory over the National Trust. He was approached by a representative in a local car park, trying to sell him membership of the charity. 'I said to him, "See all them walls that are all fallen down?" pointing to t' other side. He says, "Yes." I said, "You know who they belong to?" He says, "No." I says, "Well, they belong to the National Trust, and the day they put those walls back up will be the day I'll become a member." He hadn't an answer for that.'

THE NATIONAL TRUST

The National Trust's relationship with the Lake District goes back to the birth of the organisation in 1895. One of its three founders, Canon Hardwicke Rawnsley, the vicar at Crosthwaite, Keswick, had already been involved in successful campaigns to prevent a railway from being built in Borrowdale and to stop landowners closing paths on Latrigg. An inspirational speaker, he led the campaign, in 1902, to raise funds for the purchase of the 108-acre Brandelhow estate on the shores of Derwentwater, one of the charity's first land purchases. Established at a time when the relentless push for progress was threatening the country's landscapes, heritage and wildlife, the National Trust wanted to put its conservation principles into practice through the acquisition of property – land and buildings that could then be preserved for the entire nation in perpetuity.

The facts and figures today are astounding. Now Europe's largest conservation charity, the Trust manages about 20 per cent of the Lake District National Park – from the bed of England's deepest lake, Wastwater, to the summit of its highest mountain, Scafell Pike. Its portfolio includes huge expanses of the high fells, 24 lakes and tarns, much of Borrowdale and Langdale, various valley heads and dozens of listed buildings. It also has about 90 tenanted farms which, it is said, are home to more than two-thirds of the world's population of Herdwick sheep.

ALASTAIR'S STORY

For Alastair Young, an 18-year-old apprentice at British Nuclear Fuels' Sellafield site, joining Joss on his LMW attempt was a once-in-a-lifetime event. Now preparing to retire from Sellafield, it's an experience he's never forgotten.

'I'd never run with him before,' he says. 'I only knew him through work. Of course, everyone knew who he was; he was very respected by all the apprentices. We had the instructors like Alan Jackman and Dave Elliott tutoring us, but Joss worked in the instruments stores, so he was an adult but not one of the "teachers" – an ally and a friend. Whenever anybody went to the stores to get something, you'd linger a bit longer and have a chat with him because he was a really good crack. He was a colourful character, and he encouraged all of us to take up running.'

Alastair, who is still a member of Cumberland Athletic Club, joined Joss at Coniston Water and was supposed to run just one section with him. 'But the driver who was supposed to meet us with my clothes didn't turn up – probably because we were running ahead of time – so I carried on to Waterhead. Jogging towards Ambleside, I was gasping and out of breath. I could hardly hold a conversation, but Joss was telling me about sheep farming and his family and stuff. I certainly enjoyed the chat as we went along, but I remember thinking, "I'm just here for company really, I'm not pace-setting".

'Joss was running along, enjoying it all – going at a good, steady pace. I was overawed with how easily and effortlessly he did it considering how much ground he'd already covered and how much more he had to do. He'd rarely stop – just occasionally for a drink, a bite to eat, a massage. But then he'd be up and off again. I'd think, "If I sit down, I'm not going to be able to get up again".'

Like many of the support team who'd taken part throughout the day, Alastair also travelled to Over Water to watch Joss finish. 'It was amazing to watch him coming in at the end. It was dark and everyone was there with torches. I was fairly exhausted by that stage – it was late at night and I'd done those couple of hours' running with him earlier in the day – and I remember wondering how the devil he'd managed to do all this. He just kept going like a machine.'

Alastair, who has taken part in several half-marathons and has twice completed the London Marathon, regards himself as a road runner but, like many, is in awe of Joss's fell-running achievements. Looking back at the LMW, he adds: 'It was great to join Joss that day; everybody felt they were taking part in something really significant.'

STAGE 5

Start North-west shore of Coniston Water at end of Lake Road, Coniston (SD 308 970)

Finish Bridge over River Brathay at Skelwith Bridge (NY 344 033)

Distance 9.2 miles (14.8km)

Ascent 1070ft (326m)

Approximate walking time 4hr–4hr 30min

- Head north-east along the shore path of **Coniston Water** for 275 metres. Cross the footbridge over **Yewdale Beck** and then follow the path/lane to the **B5285**. Cross over and turn right along the shared-use path. After 0.5 miles (800 metres), turn right along the road signed for **Monk Coniston**. You'll see a path signposted to Tarn Hows and Monk Coniston on the left. Ignore this; instead take the next path on the left – fenced at first. On entering a meadow, bear left, along the field edge. Beyond the next kissing-gate, the path winds its way up through some woodland, climbing two flights of steps along the way.

- Having dropped on to a surfaced lane near Rowlandson Ground, turn left and then left again at a minor road. Go right at the next T-junction and follow the **B5285** for 0.9 miles (1.5km). Soon after passing the last building in **Hawkshead Hill**, go through the kissing-gate on your right and bear left, up the grassy slope (south-east). After crossing a farm track, continue on the faint path, passing to the left of a solitary tree. Beyond a kissing-gate, drop down the steps, over a tiny bridge and then a larger one. Bear left. After the next gate, you're on a more obvious path. Watch for two gates on the right – a farm gate with a smaller one beside it. Although the temptation is to keep left here, go through the pedestrian gate. One more gate, and you're out in a field, following the fence on your left downhill.

- Turn left along Vicarage Lane. This emerges opposite the Beatrix Potter Gallery in the centre of **Hawkshead**. (The route returns to this point after visiting Esthwaite Water.) Turn right and then keep straight ahead. At a road junction, with the old grammar school on the right, continue straight on and do the same at the next junction. Having left the village, and just after passing a narrow lane on the right, turn left along Waterside House's access lane. Nearing the house, go through the kissing-gate on the left and continue in the same direction as before. After the next set of gates, swing right and make your way south-east to the shores of **Esthwaite Water**.

- Retrace your steps to **Hawkshead**. As you see the Beatrix Potter Gallery on your right again, continue straight on to the junction with the **B5285**. Turn left here and then, in 0.3 miles (480 metres), turn left for Hawkshead Hill and Coniston. Just 185 metres beyond this junction, bear right along a narrow lane. At the next set of buildings, go through the kissing-gate on the right. A faint trail heads roughly north across the field. After a gate and bridge, head north-north-west up the slope. Beyond the kissing-gate at the top, swing north-north-east, soon picking up a semblance of a track. Near the solitary cottage at Fellfield, join a rough vehicle track and follow this to a road.

- Turn left and, after 0.3 miles (480 metres), go right. At the T-junction, turn right again and follow this road for a further 0.3 miles (480 metres). Turn left into the driveway of **Sunny Brow Farm** and immediately go through the large gate over to the right. After the next gate, bear left at a fork. The bridleway skirts the base of the partially wooded slopes of **Black Fell** and emerges at a bend on a minor road. Turn left here. Having followed the road for 0.4 miles (644 metres), turn left for Skelwith and Ambleside. Bear right when the lane forks – signposted Skelwith Bridge; you're later joined by a road coming down from the right. At the junction with the **A593**, turn right – effectively continuing straight on – to reach the River Brathay at **Skelwith Bridge**.

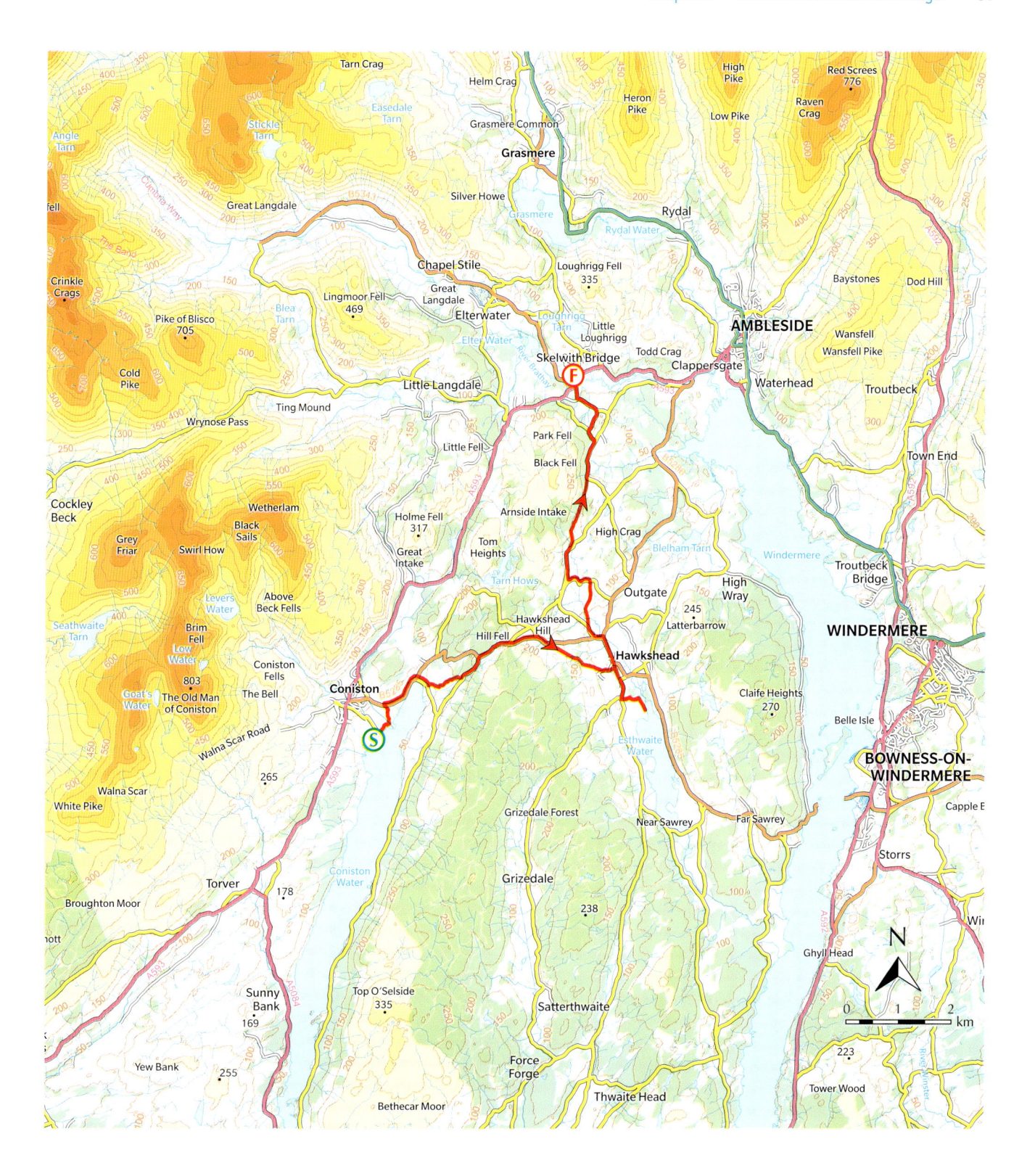

Chapter 5 – Coniston to Skelwith Bridge   81

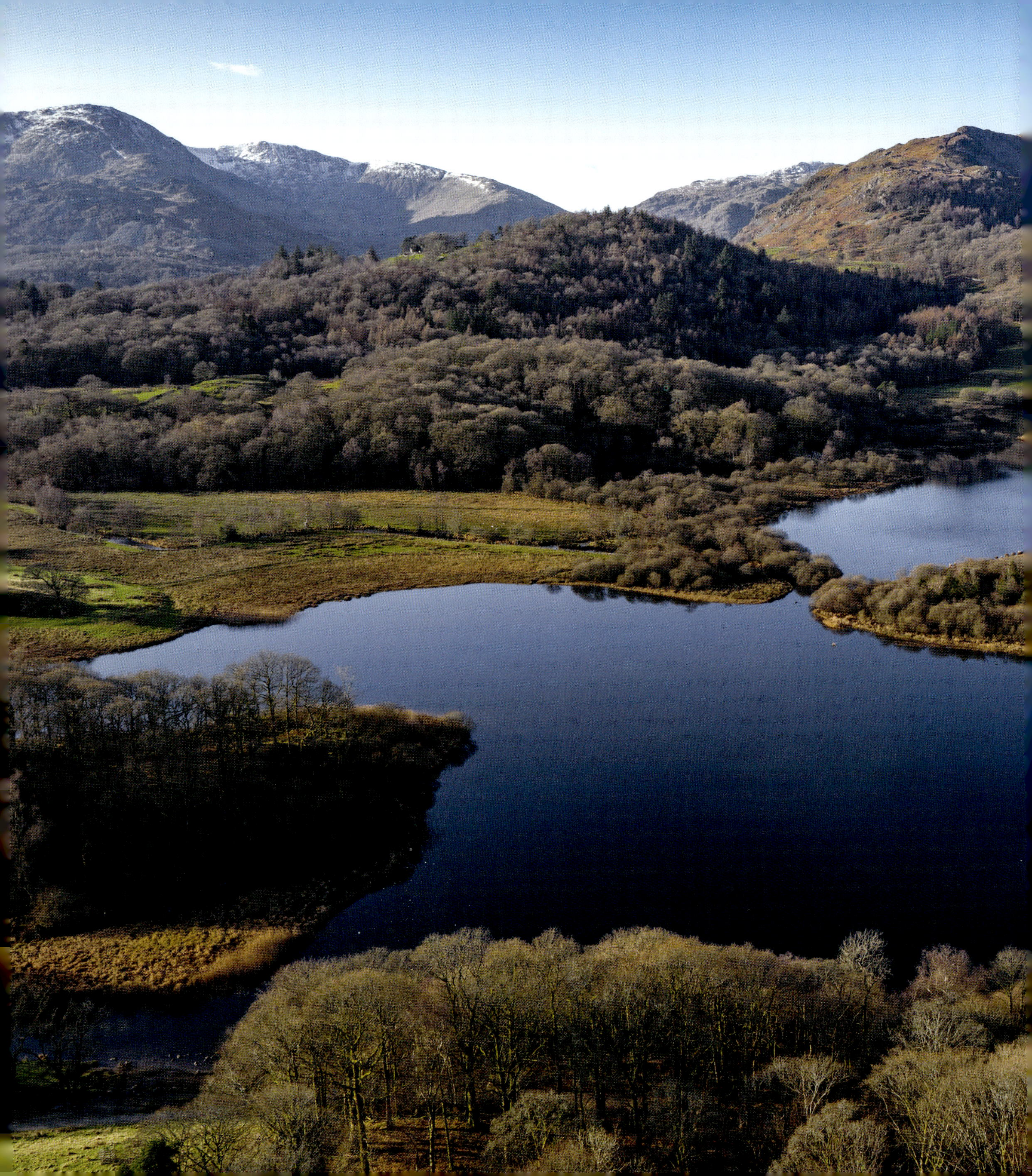

CHAPTER 6
Skelwith Bridge to Troutbeck
(Elter Water, Grasmere, Rydal Water, Windermere)

As he bounded along the riverside path from Skelwith Bridge, Joss barely had time even to register Skelwith Force. In his defence, the waterfall wasn't at its finest; it rarely is in the middle of summer. It's not a massive drop by Lakeland standards – little more than 16ft – but it does pack a punch to the senses after heavy rain as the broad, raging River Brathay forces its way through a suddenly narrower, rocky channel. It is fed by the becks that flow out of Little Langdale and Great Langdale – water with a fine pedigree, having fallen as rain on some of Lakeland's most majestic peaks, including Bow Fell, Crinkle Crags, Wetherlam and the iconic Langdale Pikes. There's a brief moment of respite as the becks reach flatter ground east of the village of Elterwater. Here they catch their breath, spread out to form a lake and then, strengthened by their newfound unity, continue downstream, over the waterfall and eventually out to Windermere.

Langdale Pikes or no Langdale Pikes, it was time to push on...

It was early afternoon when Joss emerged from the trees beside Skelwith Force and flew across the meadows just below Elter Water. Beyond the reeds to the west, he could see the slopes of Lingmoor Fell, but it was the impressive summits straight ahead that captured his attention as he quickly reached down to dip his fingers in the lake...The Langdale Pikes might not be the highest of fells – the biggest of the bunch, Harrison Stickle, is just 2414ft (736m) above sea level – but they are among the most recognisable in the whole of the Lake District, their massive crags and buttresses looming over the spectacular valley from which they take their collective name. The time was now 13:10, and things were going exceptionally well for Joss – he was an hour and 10 minutes ahead of schedule. Still, there was no way he was going to rest on his laurels; Langdale Pikes or no Langdale Pikes, it was time to push on...

'After Elter Water, there was a bit of an unsure place – I had me head down and mebbe didn't tek enough in,' he recalls. 'But somehow, I must've gotten into this field when I should've been on the road to get over Red Brow [Red Bank] and into Grasmere. I must've

◂ Aerial view of Elter Water

▲ The summer of 2020 and Joss dips his hand in Grasmere

had a blank moment. Just for a few seconds, I thought: "Where the hell am I?" And then I saw the Langdale Pikes again through a break in the trees and heard a car going up the road. I thought: "Well, that must be the road that teks us up on to Red Brow", and it did.' Picturing the exact moment in his mind, he adds: 'Just the way the sun was shining, the Pikes looked really near, as if they were on top of you. At first, I thought: "What the hell's that?" And then I had a better look. I wasn't expecting to see 'em again after the lake, but it was a perfect point that gave us a view straight through – it's fairly direct. It's a shot that's very rarely seen.' As quickly as the imposing scene had appeared though, it vanished as Joss pushed on. 'The

▲ Grasmere, lake and village

trees took the view away. Then, I dropped down through the woods, touched Grasmere lake and went over the bank till Rydal Water.'

He wouldn't have hung around chatting with tourists back in 1983, but revisiting Grasmere and Rydal Water at a more leisurely pace 37 years later allows him to chew the cud with anyone and everyone. Families with children always make his eyes light up. 'With all the paths they've put in now, these places are good for families to get out and spend the day,' he says as we stroll along Loughrigg Terrace, with its spectacular views across the water and up to the notch of Dunmail Raise. 'You pack the sandwiches and tek the kids with you.' Even more likely to add to the sparkle in his eyes are the dogs we encounter. As we near Rydal Water, a tiny, white ball of joyful fluff – probably a bichon frise – runs excitedly between our legs. Joss stands and watches, laughing, as it shoots up and down the slopes bordering the path. It occasionally disappears into the bracken, but never seems to make much progress among the dense tangle.

Joss has always had dogs – from a child on the family farm at Wasdale Head right up until he moved to Gosforth, when he had to ask his friend Sheila to provide a larger, more suitable home for

▲ Rydal Water in winter

his current dog Lassie. On the farm at Bowderdale, he always had a pack of about six dogs that worked with his sheep, usually collies or collie crosses, as well as a terrier; and he continued to keep at least a few dogs when he moved to Greendale. Scamp, Patch, Sam, Titch, Moss, Spy, Fly, Nip the terrier, Gyp, Bell, Smart and Chance were among the dogs, hard-working and otherwise, that formed part of the Naylor clan down the years. And then there was the incomparable Lassie, who could go 'flat out' all day on the fells and of whom the sheep were 'bloody terrified'. Joss always claims that Lassie died of a broken heart because she could no longer work; just two days after being retired due to disc problems in her back, she was gone. His current Lassie, he says, has no such qualms about being retired and is now 'spoilt rotten' by a life of leisure as a pet. She never was the best of sheepdogs, he admits, but was 'good for going to t' tops with' because she had 'a lot of bark'.

From Rydal Water, Joss 'legged on' towards Windermere

Other than Richard Eastman's aforementioned Juno though, with its 'bloody great arsehole staring back' at Joss all the way from Devoke Water to Goat's Water, no dogs accompanied the runners on the LMW.

From Rydal Water, Joss 'legged on' towards Windermere. After dropping towards the humpback Pelter Bridge, beside the A591, he ran the Under Loughrigg lane, which follows the Rothay downstream. This is the river that flows between Grasmere and Rydal Water before joining up with the River Brathay to enter Windermere at Waterhead. 'There was about a mile of road to run till Windermere. It's further than you think, but it's a nice quiet little road.'

Joss was running with Alan Jackman now – like Dave Elliott, an instructor at Sellafield at the time, but sadly no longer with us. 'Alan got into running through doing half-marathons at work. He was a

Joss touched the shores of Windermere at Waterhead ▲

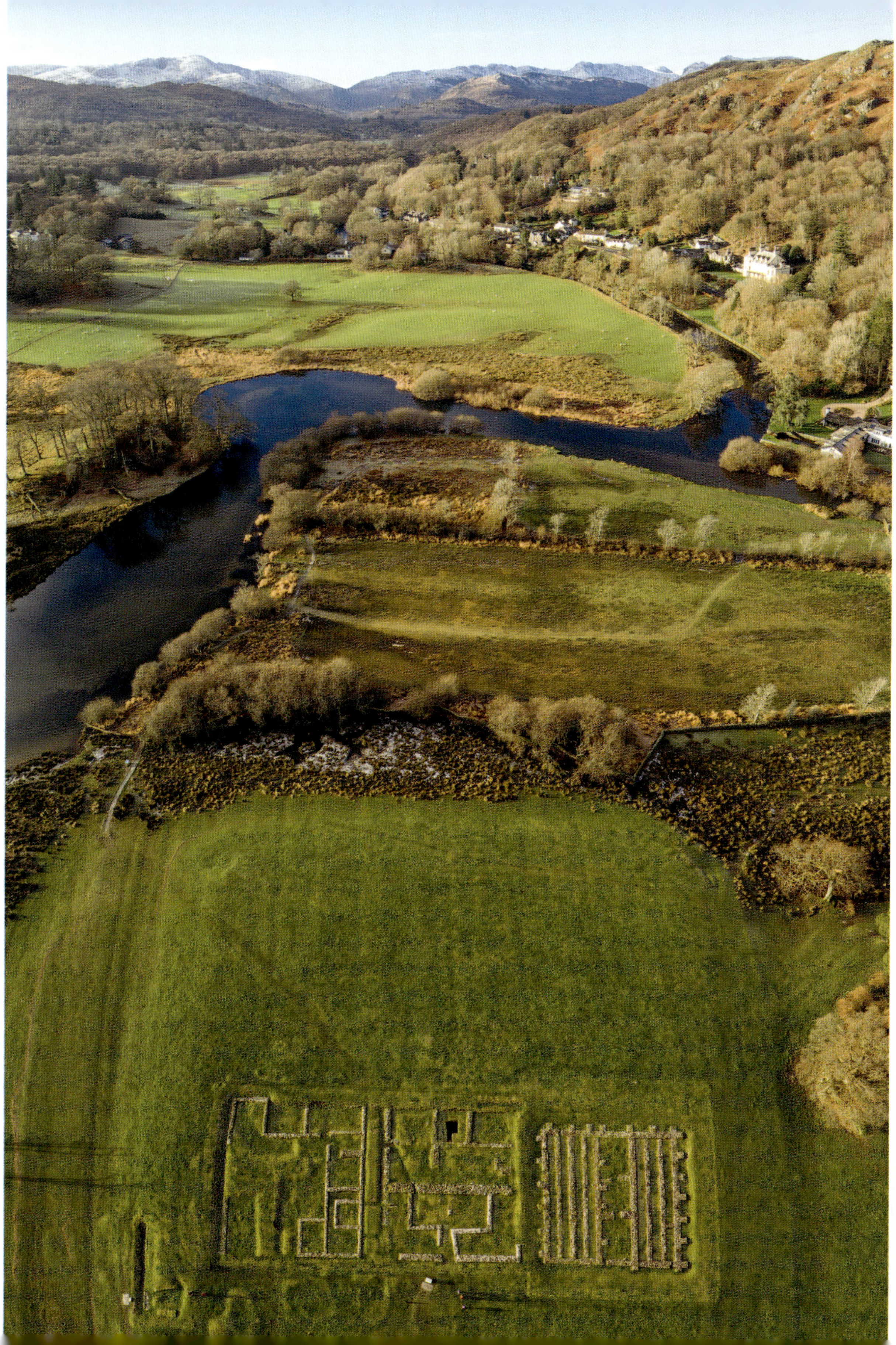

good, middle-of-the-field runner, and got to be quite strong – a handy lad. On odd nights, if we had nowt on, we'd go for a run together. He did a fair stretch with us on that day – he was running well.'

Alan was one of several runners who joined Joss on the LMW, acting not just as pacemakers but as companions during the long hours spent on the 105-mile route. Joss frequently used to run by himself on the fells, and still loves the solitude of the hills, but he also enjoyed 'the crack' of running with others. 'There's a point comes when you need company, but it's got to be someone you can confide in – someone that you know you can tell 'em summat and that's it, it won't go no further.' He adds that he often chatted 'a fair bit' on the LMW unless he was covering 'serious ground'. 'It was good to have someone new to talk to – a change of crack.' Alan ran the longest section with him – a stint of more than seven-and-a-half hours from Coniston Water to Brothers Water – but most of the other runners stayed for just two or three hours.

When Joss finally reached England's longest lake, number 15 on his 27-strong itinerary, it was not quite 2pm, and he was an hour and 25 minutes ahead of his estimates. Expecting to meet up with members of his support team, who would have dry shoes and socks waiting for him, he decided to cool off in the lake while waiting for them. 'There was neebody there, so I went and stood in the water to cool me feet off – up to me knees.' After 10 minutes of this, there was still no sign of the support team. 'So I just said, "Bugger this, there's neebody coming; I'll go round by the road". When I was looking at the route the weekend before, I was gonna go up into the woods. It's a nice run up there to Troutbeck Windermere, but I had to miss that out; I went round by Low Wood Bay instead. It put another mile or two on, and the water was coming out of me socks and me shoes, but it was all right – it got lighter as I went on. And just as I got to the top to drop into Troutbeck Windermere, the car caught up with us and I got some dry socks on.'

Keen to see some of what he missed out on in 1983, Joss suggests we take a stroll along Robin Lane when we call in at Troutbeck on our rewalking of the route in 2020. His original plan would've

▲ Old sign at Troutbeck

Harebells, foxgloves and brambles thrive beside the gravel lane

seen him loping through the sumptuous Skelghyll Wood after leaving Waterhead, past High Skelghyll Farm and then joining the old droving roads of Troutbeck. These walled lanes would once have been used almost solely for moving livestock around; today, there are probably more walkers on these byways and bridleways than there are sheep and cattle. Robin Lane, which leads up to Hundreds Road on its steady journey on to the lower slopes of Wansfell, is just one of them.

Harebells, foxgloves and brambles thrive beside the gravel lane. I comment on the blackberries that are making an early appearance this year. 'We've never heard of blackberries up here,' says Dave Elliott, gently teasing the only southerner in the group. He tells me they're 'blackites'. Despite having lived in Cumbria for nearly a quarter of a century, and having learnt many dialect words in that time, 'blackites' is one that is new to me, and I check online later just to make sure it's not a double bluff.

Joss points out a small, trough-like construction beside the lane, with water running through it, which he says would've been used by horses. Always observant, he picks up on lots of detail like this wherever we walk. He clearly takes immense pleasure not only from the natural environment, but from the man-made features of the farming landscape – and is particularly buoyed by examples of good dry-stone walling. 'That was put in properly,' he says, admiring a step stile in the wall. 'You'd think some of these walls would go any minute, but they're fine and strong,' he adds, running his hands along the stonework. 'They've used good slates, and the walls have got throughs in them.' He indicates the longer stones that extend the entire width of the wall, helping to bond the smaller stones together to provide strength and stability. Even the stump of a recently felled tree catches his attention. Although it must have been a massive tree, it was brought down, he suggests, very carefully and thoughtfully – without causing any damage to the wall beside which it grew.

The craftsmanship and care that has gone into building and then maintaining these walls is something to which Joss can relate.

◀ The recommended route passes the lakeside Roman fort of Galava, seen at the bottom of this picture

▲ Joss in a sheepfold he built at Greendale

As a farmer, he is justifiably proud of the work he has put into preserving the often ancient walls at Bowderdale and Greendale over the years. Patching them up with wire is, in his eyes, simply not good enough; each gap, created by flood water or rockfall from the fells above, needs to be skilfully rebuilt in a way that will allow the walls to survive for generations. It's part of the tradition of Lakeland farming, something that has to be upheld, both literally and figuratively.

These walls have been dividing valley bottoms and snaking up and down the steepest of fells for centuries. Some of the earliest were created by the monks of Furness Abbey, in the middle of the 13th century, when the Cistercian brothers decided to create enclosures for the livestock they farmed at Brotherilkeld in Eskdale. Irregular valley walls continued to be constructed throughout the medieval period and then, after the enclosure acts of the 18th and 19th centuries, the long, straight walls typical of the higher ground began to appear.

'They're important to the Lake District,' says Joss, standing beside a gate and placing his long, wiry fingers on one of the coping stones that provide a tidy rock crown for the walls enclosing Robin Lane. Below us, beyond the gateway, Windermere, another icon of the National Park landscape, leads off into the hazy distance. It's tempting to pause here – to rest on a bench and admire the scenery – but the valley heat is already building, and we want to complete the climb to Garburn Pass before it gets too hot for comfort.

HISTORY OF THE '26 LAKE, MERES AND WATERS'

The first round of the '26 Lake, Meres and Waters' was completed in June 1981 by Leo Pollard, later a member of Lostock Athletic Club, who did it in 35hr 29min. He enlisted the help of members of the Achille Ratti Climbing Club on his visit to the 26 bodies of water named as 'lakes', 'meres' or 'waters' on the 1958 one-inch Ordnance Survey map of the Lake District. (The club still maintains records for the round, and now presents commemorative certificates to those committed few who complete it.)

Writing about the experience later in an account for the Achille Ratti Climbing Club, Leo said the weather had been 'atrocious' on the first day, and it had 'paid off having mountaineers as pacers and route finders'. Contending with heavy rain and thick mist, even down to valley level at times, he and his pacemakers slipped on several occasions. He slid on 'greasy rocks' on the way down to Greendale Tarn and felt the first pull in his groin.

'Darkness came between Rydal Water and Windermere,' he wrote. 'It was raining heavily as we walked over the Garburn Pass, [and] as we descended into Kentmere some of the support party came up, their bright torch light being very helpful to us on such a night.' Navigating from Skeggles Water 'proved a little difficult' and 'as always when things go wrong, the heather seems to get taller and bogs deeper'. Dawn broke and the weather started improving as they made their way to Haweswater. 'At Haweswater I was feeling pretty sorry for myself, I had nursed a groin strain from Coniston Water, and the way over to Small Water, Blea Water, High Street and Hayeswater was going to be painful. I did a bit of groaning on the way up High Street and in true Graham style the lads completely ignored me.' In contrast to the previous day though, the section from Brothers Water to Over Water was completed in 'heat wave conditions' and Leo's success was eventually toasted with his son Gary's home-made wine. ('Graham' in Leo's account is a reference to the Bob Graham Round, one of the UK's classic fell-running challenges, involving the ascent of 42 Lakeland fells in 24 hours.)

Since then, only a further 13 people have completed the challenge, four of those as pairs. Alan Heaton, of Clayton-le-Moors Harriers, really upped the ante in 1982 when he finished the route in just 25hr 16min, but his record was shattered the following year by Joss, who added Kentmere Reservoir to his own personal tally. Joss's record has stood since then. The first woman was Amy Norfolk (Liverpool Running Club), who achieved a time of 42hr 59min in December 2019, while the current holder of the women's record is Kirsty Hewitson (30hr 10min in June 2021).

The most recent completion, at the time of writing, was by Rob Allen, of Keswick Athletic Club, who managed a time of 29hr 21min in December 2020 – the third fastest time and a new winter record. His own attempt was partly inspired by a chance meeting with Joss in Wasdale. 'Joss spoke in glowing terms about the route and later in a phone call confirmed that it would, in his opinion, make a great winter route given the lack of extended time on the high tops,' he says. It had always been Rob's plan to run it 'as a tribute to Joss', so he took the same route, including Kentmere Reservoir.

▲ Joss has a short rest during the LMW
(Photo credit: Dave Elliott)

STAGE 6

Start Bridge over River Brathay at Skelwith Bridge (NY 344 033)

Finish Eastern end of Robin Lane, near Old Post Office, Troutbeck (NY 407 026)

Distance 9.4 miles (15.1km)

Ascent 1700ft (518m)

Approximate walking time 4hr 30min–5hr

▶ From the bridge over the **River Brathay**, head west along the driveway leading up to Chesters By The River. Bear right when the lane forks. A riverside path heads upstream, passing **Skelwith Force** waterfall. After several meadows, the surfaced path reaches the edge of **Elter Water** and enters some woods. About 145 metres after the gate into the trees, turn right – almost back on yourself – and climb to the **B5343**. Cross diagonally right to go through a gap in the wall opposite. An indistinct, unmarked trail heads steeply uphill through the trees.

▶ After a gate in the top wall, bear left. At a junction of paths above the cottage at Crag Head, turn left. Drop on to a vehicle track and follow this to the road. Turn left and then keep right when the road splits, following signs for **High Close**. Immediately after passing (and ignoring) a road turning on the left, go through the gate on the right into Deerbolts Wood. This later emerges on **Loughrigg Terrace**. Keep to the bridleway, high above **Grasmere**, until you come to a junction of paths close to the next walled area of woodland. To visit the lake, drop left and then return to this junction. Now continue with the wall on your left, generally east, gradually dropping to the shores of **Rydal Water**.

▶ Nearing the eastern end of the lake, keep right, climbing to join a path from the right. This becomes a surfaced lane and drops to a T-junction next to Pelter Bridge, just off the A591. Turn right – along the Under Loughrigg Road. At the junction with the **A593** on the edge of **Ambleside**, cross diagonally right, through a gap in a wall opposite to join a shared cycleway/footpath. Cross the bridge over the **River Rothay** and, after the small gate on the other side, turn sharp right through a larger gate. Follow the River Rothay downstream.

▶ After the Birdhouse Meadows boardwalk, close to where the rivers Rothay and Brathay meet before they flow into Windermere, you'll enter a more open area that is home to the remains of the **Roman fort of Galava**. Head half-left and then go through

▲ Ten minutes? Three if you're Joss Naylor

one of the two pedestrian gates in the wall on the far side of the fort. In Borrans Park, join a circular path. It doesn't matter which way you go, although anti-clockwise leads to the shore of **Windermere**. Leave via the ramp in the park's north-east corner and turn right along the **A5075**.

▶ At the lit road junction, cross to the east side of the **A591** and turn left. In a few metres, climb the steps straight ahead (not the ones on the right) to join a footpath climbing right. After a wall stile, head south-east across an open area. A small ladder stile provides access to a woodland trail, continuing uphill. At a three-way split, go straight across, soon stepping up on to a wider path. Turn right here, into the heart of **Skelghyll Wood**.

▶ About 160 metres beyond the farmyard at **High Skelghyll**, go through the gate on the left to join a rising path. At the top of this, veer right along Robin Lane. This eventually drops to **Troutbeck**, next to the Old Post Office café.

Chapter 6 – Skelwith Bridge to Troutbeck 93

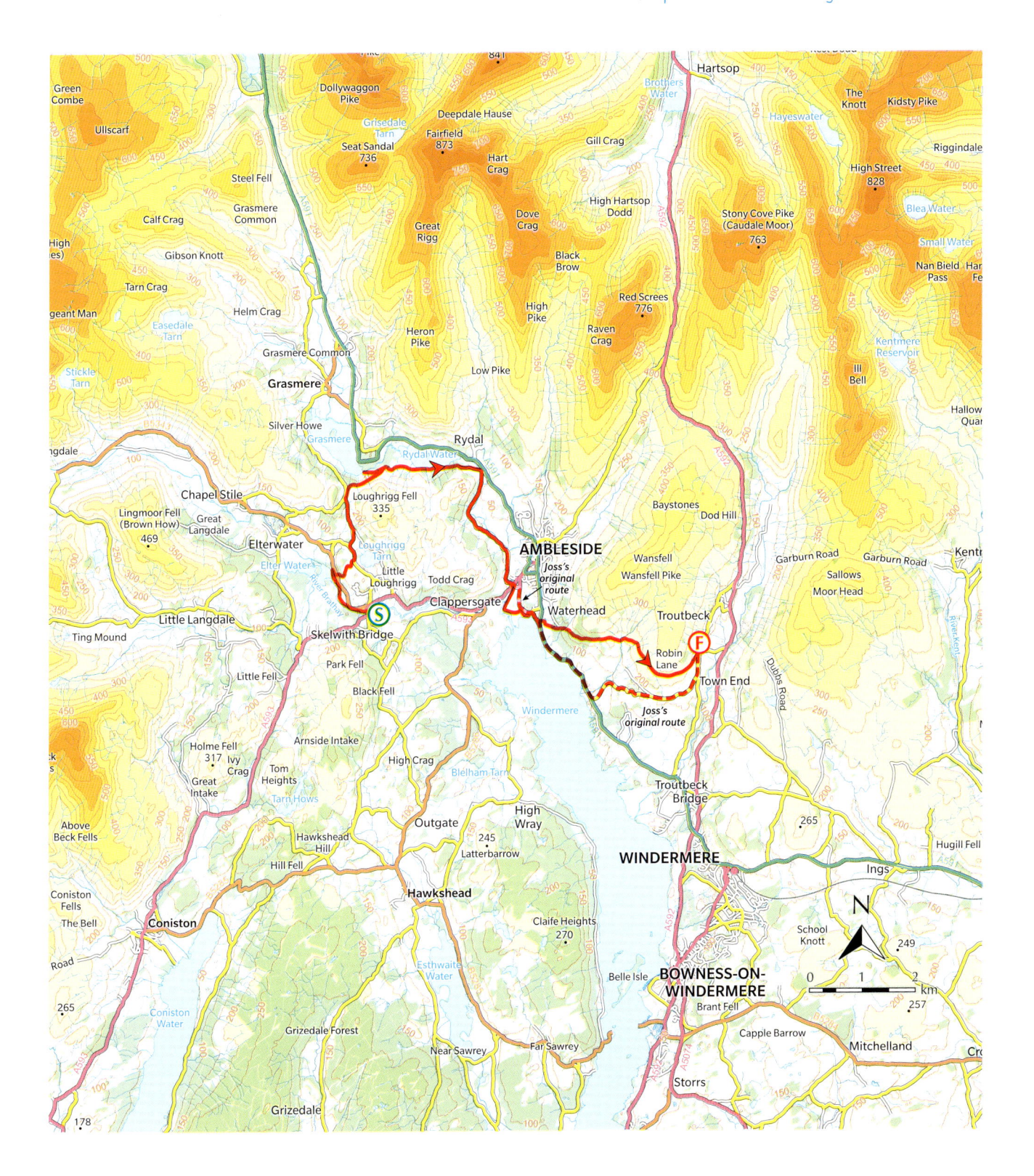

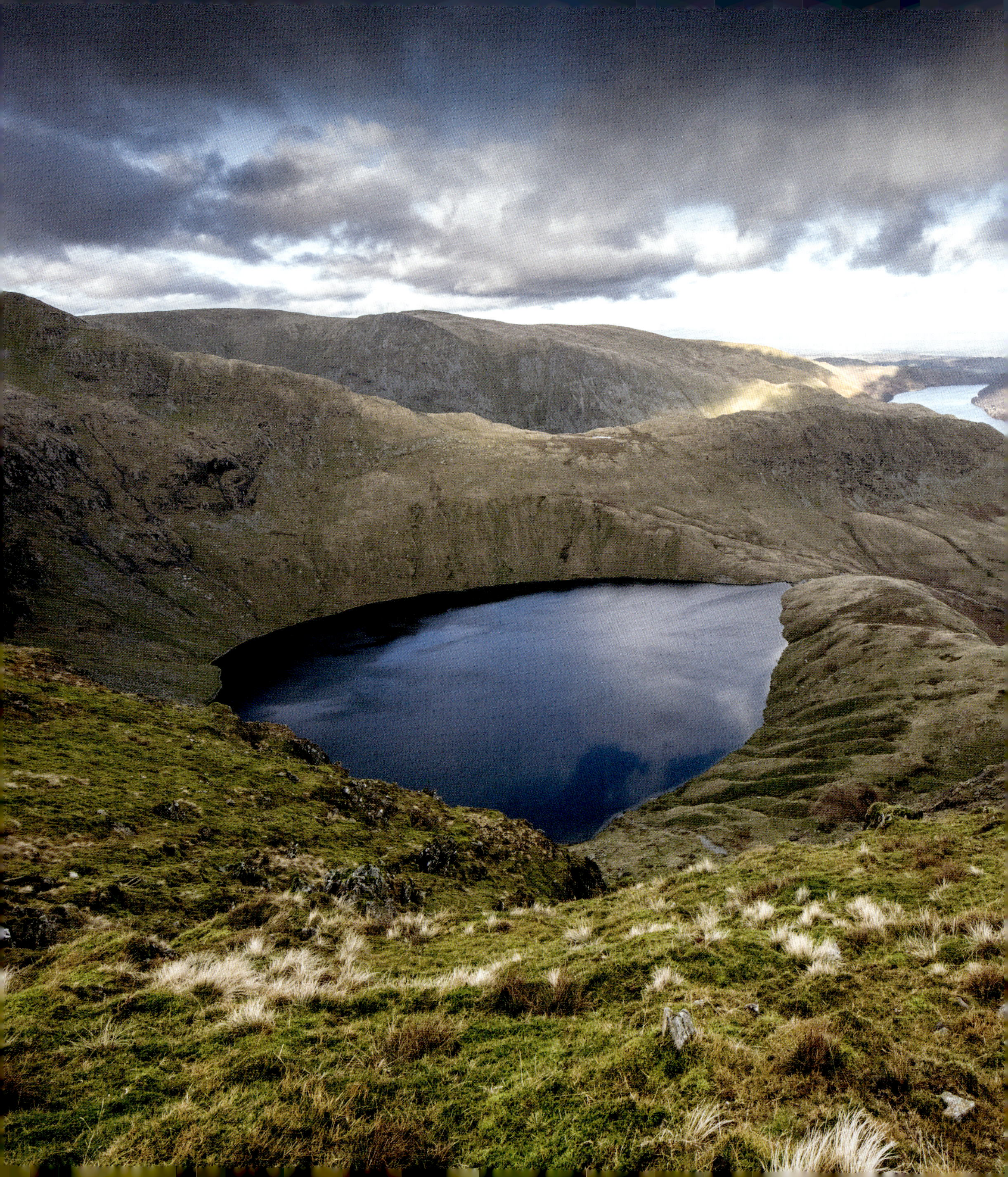

CHAPTER 7
Troutbeck to Haweswater
(Skeggles Water, Kentmere Reservoir, Small Water, Blea Water)

It was uncomfortably hot as Joss climbed the Garburn Road from Troutbeck. The searing heat and the bright sunlight were bouncing off the slate on the track, hitting him in the face, and there wasn't a breath of wind. The gradient wasn't too punishing though, and he managed to maintain his easy, steady pace. To the west, the traditional cottages and farmhouses of the village were strung out in a long row above the valley floor. Dating back to medieval times, the settlement was built along a line of springs and, externally at least, has probably changed little in the intervening centuries. Directly above it, the slopes of Wansfell, parcelled into higgledy-piggledy enclosures known as The Hundreds, added to the sense of having been transported back in time.

The views of the western arm of the Kentmere Horseshoe, the ring of high fells that encloses the upper reaches of Kentmere, were hazy, although the shapely Ill Bell rose above it all. It was like a child's drawing of a mountain – a simple, almost-flawless pyramid. The only thing missing was the wavy, drawn line of snow topping. I suggest a little patch of cooling snow wouldn't have gone amiss that flaming June day. 'Aye, it was hot, even hotter than this,' Joss confirms as we retrace his steps in 2020. As we gain height, we pick

▲ Jesus Church at Troutbeck

◀ The perfect teardrop of Blea Water, with Haweswater visible below

up the faintest hint of a breeze. 'I can handle that!' he exclaims, adding that there was no such relief in 1983.

'I'd been this way a few times before when I'd been running, and there's a little spring that comes down the back of a wall up there.' He indicates vaguely, waving a walking pole at an indeterminate spot higher up the track. 'I stopped with Alan and had a mouthful from it. It was good – sweet water.' He begins chuckling as he remembers another hot day when he'd been out running with his son-in-law Peter Ferris, and they'd had a nasty surprise after drinking from the same spring. 'I says to Peter, "Let's just stop here and have a drink." I got down to have a drink; he got down to have a drink. And I says to him, "That water tasted a bit strange as though there was summat in it." So I looked over the wall and, in 't next field, there was four cows standing in the gutter, having a drink, and one of them had shit in 't water.' I pull a face, and Joss laughs again. 'I'd drunk there a few times before though. It just adds to the flavour, doesn't it?' We try to find 'Cowshit Beck' later, but its exact location eludes us.

▲ Joss on the old byway

'That water tasted a bit strange as though there was summat in it'

It's a surprisingly quiet day, with few other people on the stony track. Even the birds seem to have abandoned the open areas, choosing to hide out in the shade. The lack of birdlife disturbs Joss – until we see a single group of meadow pipits flitting about just ahead, always staying a few yards in front of us. 'A family of them!' Joss exclaims, joyfully. 'At Greendale, they used to come into our 10-acre meadow. There'd be 30 or 40 of them. They'd be there till June or July and then they'd tek off.'

Commenting on the lack of human company on a hot, sunny day in the increasingly popular Lake District, he says: 'We're lucky, ain't we? It's surprising, you can go places and expect it to be busy, but then you don't see a soul.' It's only when we get to the top of the Garburn Pass that we see the first people since leaving the valley bottom. Three young teenagers are wheeling their heavily laden bikes up from Kentmere. The first to appear is a little reticent – either shy, or wary of strangers – but then the group's 'spokesman' catches up, keen to answer all the questions fired at him. It turns out they're visiting from south-west London, having caught the train up from Euston to Oxenholme and then Windermere. They had intended to cycle as far as Angle Tarn to camp the previous night but were forced to stop at Kentmere Reservoir because they'd found it such hard work. They were now on their way to Grasmere. They talk

Chapter 7 – Troutbeck to Haweswater 97

▲ Looking down the Garburn Road to Troutbeck

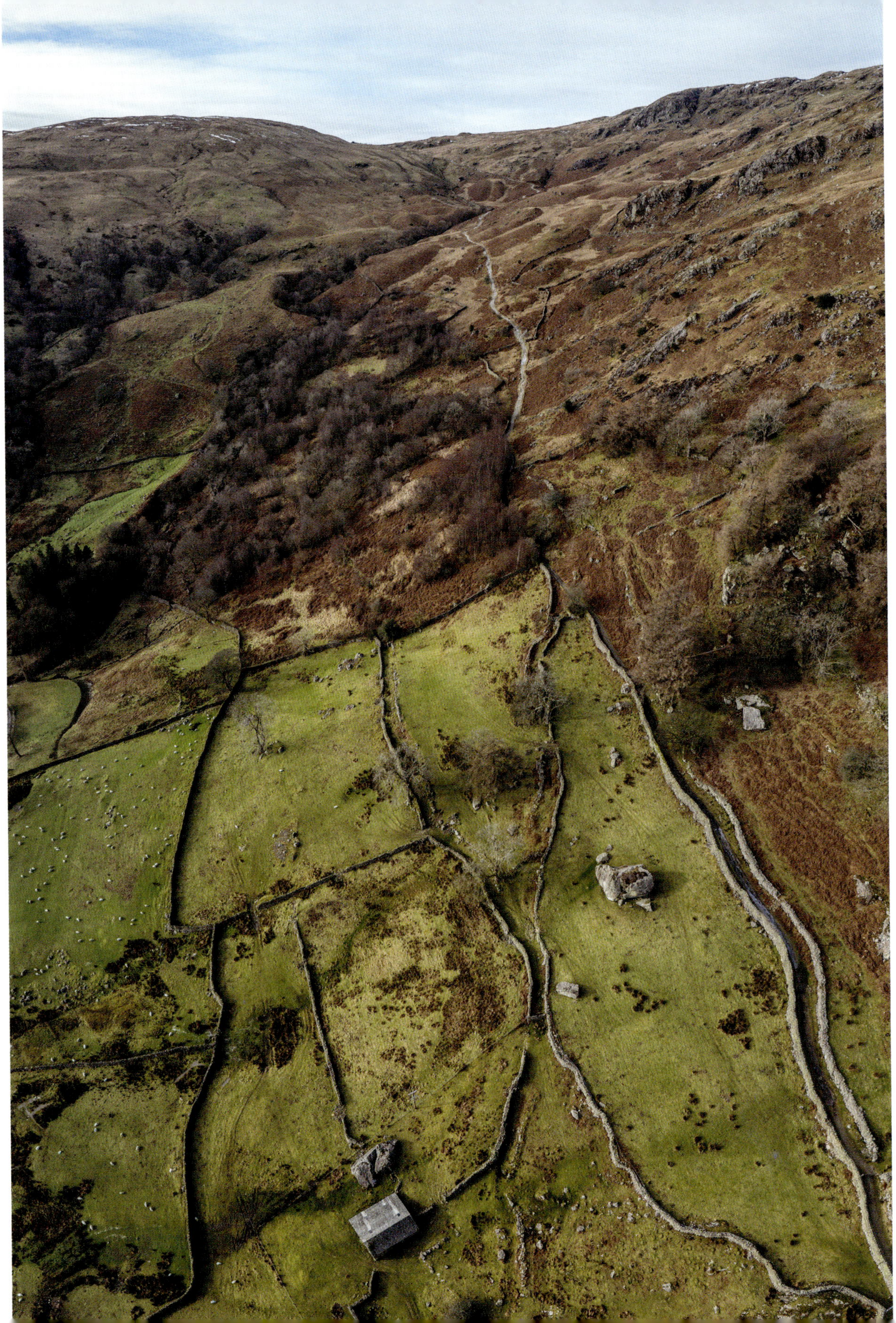

enthusiastically about how they've already visited the South Downs and the Brecon Beacons with the Scouts, and now want to explore further afield. This is their first trip to the Lakes and, when pressed, they confirm they're loving it. 'When we're older, we want to go to Scotland.' Such youthful simplicity coupled with their ardour for being outdoors brings smiles to the faces of everyone in our group.

Smiles then turn to big, cheesy grins as the quietest in the group asks: 'Will there be any dustbins down in Grasmere? We've got a load of rubbish we need to get rid of.' He indicates a large, black bag strapped to the back of his bike. During one of the busiest summers the Lake District has ever seen, the subject of 'fly' campers and 'dirty' campers leaving huge volumes of litter all over the National Park has come up frequently as we've rewalked the LMW, causing frustration, anger and sometimes despair. Suddenly though, with one simple encounter, all that negativity is temporarily forgotten.

As the three young Londoners push on, completely oblivious to the uplifting effect they've had on our group, Joss leaps on to a rock outcrop. 'Good viewpoint this!' he exclaims and begins to point out the route ahead. After dropping into Kentmere valley on his original run, he headed out to Skeggles Water. From there, things get confusing. He'd always wanted to include Kentmere Reservoir on the round even though it wasn't in Leo Pollard's original list of 26. (The dale's original mere was further downstream, close to what is now little more than a wide spot on the River Kent known as Kentmere Tarn, but he felt the 'mere' in the valley's name still needed to be acknowledged.) How was he going to reach the reservoir from Skeggles Water though?

'I had big intentions of going up Longsleddale, over till Haweswater and then dropping back into Kentmere from Blea Water and Small Water.' This immediately raises a few eyebrows, as it did, apparently, among the marshals back in 1983. There was no digital mapping, no clever software nor complicated spreadsheets to help Joss plan his route back then, so it was all done with traditional paper maps.

'When you look on the map, it is a shorter distance to go up Longsleddale to Haweswater,' suggests Pete.

'Aye, that's right,' says Joss.

'But you'd have to come back. To me, it would've been daft to go to Haweswater first,' Pete adds.

'Aye, that's why I changed my mind; I thought it'd be faster if I dropped back in [to Kentmere] from Skeggles. It's an old packhorse path in the valley; nice running. It's not many minutes and you'd be out of there.'

From the top of the Garburn Pass though, Joss's next move would've been in no doubt – still on the old road, he descended directly into Kentmere. 'The track was chewed up real bad when I came through,' he recalls. 'It was getting a hammering because there were a lot of four-by-fours using it. And there were motorbikes too – young fellas scrambling and digging it up. I think they've stopped them all now; it'd got too much.' In 1983, the Garburn Road was still classified as a 'byway', meaning that any vehicle could use it. Since then though, new laws have enabled it to be reclassified as a 'restricted byway' so that only non-motorised vehicles have access to it.

Over the wall to the south, he saw Kentmere Hall, with its 14th-century pele tower. Sporting walls that are 5ft thick, this stronghold would've provided refuge for the wealthy Gilpin family in the event of Scottish raids on the valley. Joss's rapid descent ended just after the church of St Cuthbert, but he barely had time to register the level ground of the valley bottom before he began his climb out the other side.

Following another walled lane – this one grassier and more comfortable underfoot than the routes in and out of Troutbeck – he freed a pair of lambs that had been trapped in a fence. 'They'd been playing, and they'd both run into this wire and were hanging with their feet through it. They hadn't been trapped too long, like, but they were only about four months old, so they would've soon deteriorated. I came over the wall and pulled 'em out. They seemed quite pleased to be freed.'

There are hardly any sheep around when we visit Kentmere a week after our wanderings in and around Troutbeck, but we are lucky enough to spot some wildlife. Cutting a corner on the path to maintain height, Joss briefly goes off-piste. As he darts over a small outcrop, he disturbs a buzzard that casually lifts off the rock and, with two flaps of its massive wings, glides away. Five seconds later, as I pass beneath the same rock, I inadvertently flush out a hare. It suddenly shoots out from among the tussocks, almost from beneath my feet, and races away. 'A hare!' Joss exclaims with genuine, child-like joy.

It's not long before we see Skeggles Water ahead, a shallow body of water sitting rather forlornly on the uninspiring moorland shelf. There were once plans to drain Skeggles Water to extract the rare diatomite that lies beneath its surface. Almost pure silica, this soft sedimentary rock is used in filters, adhesives, paint and insulation products.

Skeggles Water is probably the least-known body of water on the entire route, and even Joss has only seen it two or three times in

> 'A hare!' Joss exclaims with genuine, child-like joy

◀ Drone shot of the Garburn Road as it drops to Kentmere

Kentmere, with the high fells ranged around the reservoir ▶▶

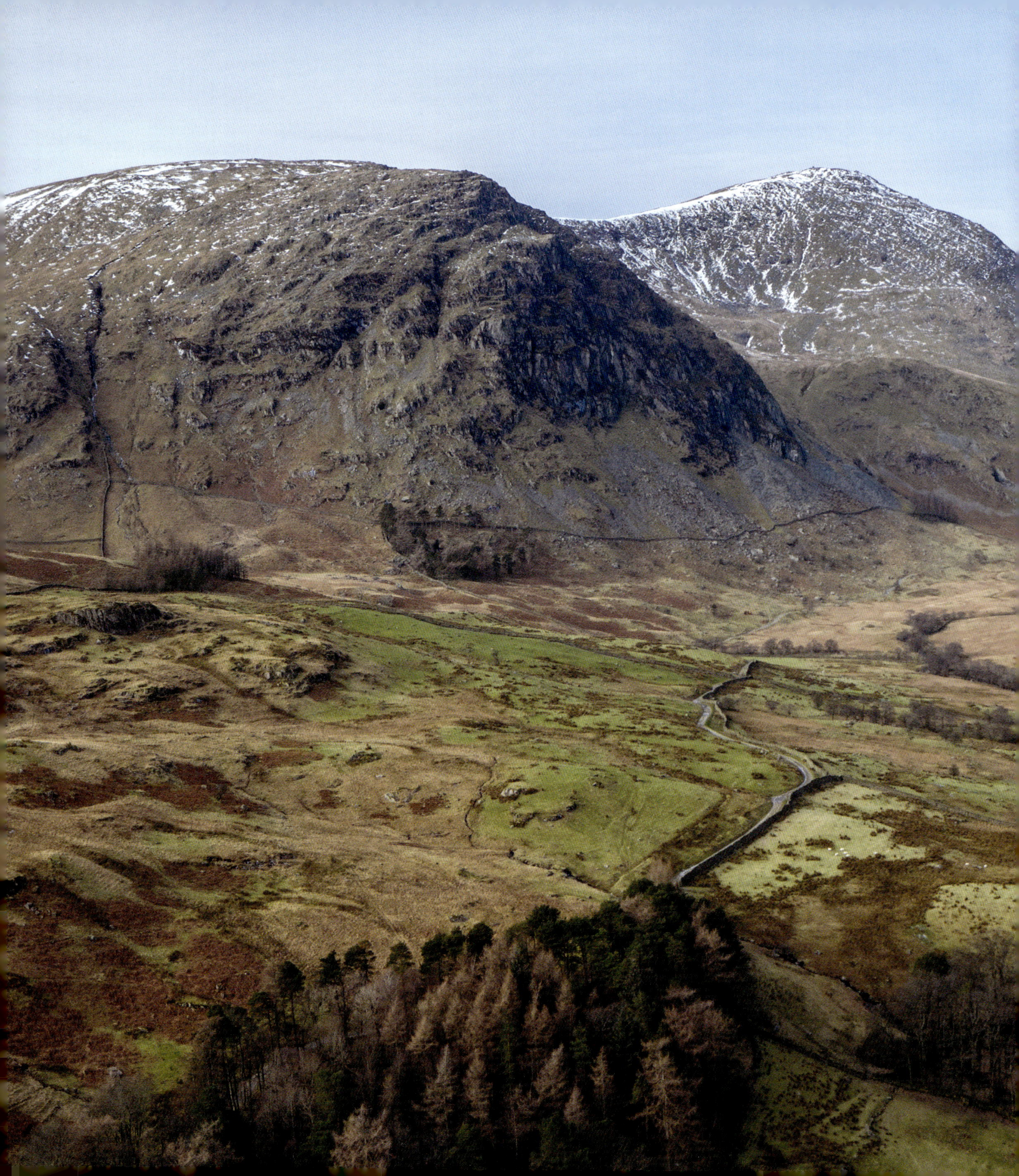

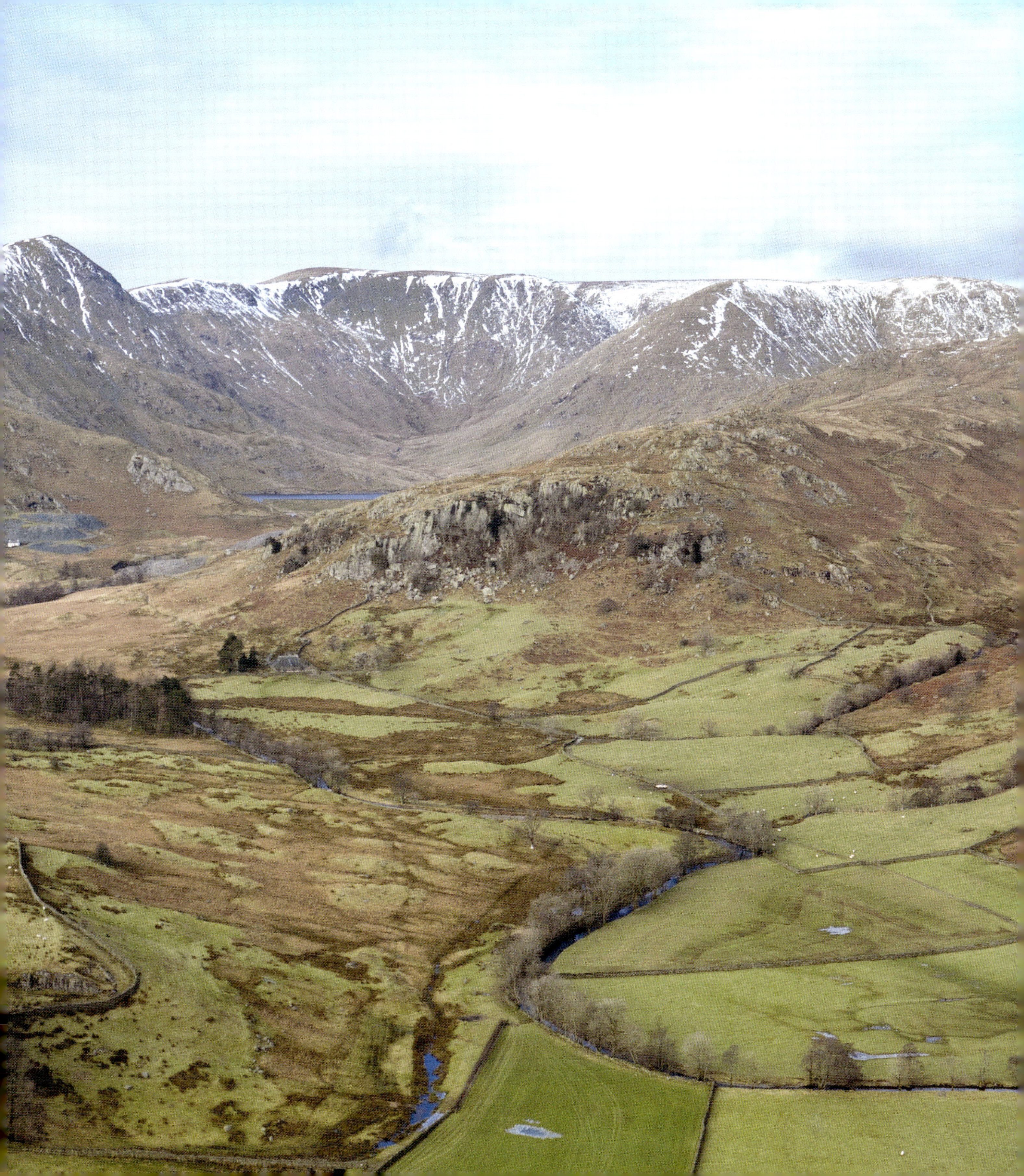

his entire life. I suggest that no one would've missed it if it had been drained. 'Probably not!' Joss replies, laughing. 'I don't think many people visit it. You see these places where people never go, but there aren't many left now.' He says he wasn't particularly taken by the tarn when he saw it on his LMW attempt, but admits there is something appealing about it today, surrounded by a carpet of purple heather. 'Them sort of places are nice to visit because you only go there mebbe once or twice in a lifetime. That's what makes it [the LMW] so special.' As we wade through the heather, the flowers release a light dusting of pollen that hovers just above the ground, filling the air with its sweet, slightly cloying smell. Standing at the water's edge, Joss points out the pathless route he took away from the tarn, climbing north across rough ground with only a wall for company.

There was rough, tussocky ground to negotiate all around Skeggles Water, the sort of terrain where, as a runner, Joss was glad to have someone as experienced as Alan accompanying him. 'On stuff like that, you need to have someone with you who knows what they're doing.' The ability to read the ground ahead was absolutely vital – to anticipate every potentially ankle-twisting lump and bump without having to slow down. And there was no chance that Joss was going to slow down. Although he'd lost some of the massive advantage he'd built up earlier in the day, it was still only 16:03 when he reached the tarn, against a projected time of 17:10. Andrew Simpson, one of the marshals who met him there, armed with cake and juice, remembers he was 'gone quicker than he arrived', pausing for just a matter of seconds.

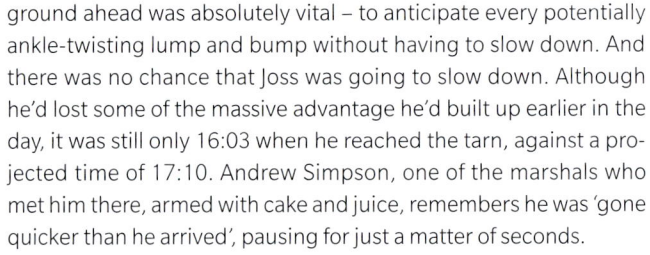

Back in the valley bottom, the hay-making was in full flow. 'Aye, the lads were busy that day,' says Joss, referring to the farm workers in the fields. 'It's very fertile, the ground in the bottom there.' As he's telling me this, we round a corner to see some young men loading bales of silage on to a trailer. Although some hay meadows, because of their biodiversity, have been restored in the north of England in recent years, silage (fermented grass) has replaced hay as a winter feed on almost all livestock farms. While you need five or six days of dry weather to make hay, silage requires a much smaller weather window. Heading up the valley in a short while, we spot a farm on the opposite side of the valley. 'That's where those lads'll be taking them,' says Joss, indicating the enormous pile of bales near the farmhouse, ready to meet demand for feed during the coming winter.

'There aren't many valleys like this, unspoilt and with the old packhorse route still going straight up it,' says Joss as we make our way up towards Kentmere Reservoir. 'It's nice that the walls are looked after too. In some places, beside the old roads, they're just let go.' While lamenting the lack of care taken over some walls, he makes a beeline for one section that he's just spotted. The through stones show prominently at regular intervals. He insists Stephen takes a photo. 'These are proper walls.'

Nearing the head of the valley, the fells begin crowding in around us again. For Joss in 1983, this marked the moment of his return to more rugged fell country. Since leaving Coniston five hours earlier, he'd passed through fairly benign countryside, but this was a lot more dramatic, particularly to the west where rocky slopes reared up abruptly. Yoke, a nondescript fell when you pass over the top of it, looked dark and ominous from the valley floor, the rocks of Rainsborrow Crag almost black. An apron of boulders spilled from a yawning quarry mouth.

Beyond Tongue Close, the path narrowed and hugged the banks of the River Kent. Joss remembers this being fairly sedate back in 1983, but, following a series of slow-moving electrical storms, the water level is high and moving at a tremendous pace when we encounter it. We've quickly gone from a scene of pastoral tranquillity to something altogether more serious.

> **The ability to read the ground ahead was absolutely vital**

▲ On the moorland near Skeggles Water

One of the marshals at Kentmere Reservoir was Phil Atherton, another of the many Sellafield apprentices Dave had roped in to help on the day. He remembers the moment Joss 'came over the hill with Alan Jackman and dropped down to "skop a pebble in 't lake".' Joss jokingly asked Phil if he wanted to join him on the next section. 'My face must've been a picture as I had walking boots on and was not kit out for running at all,' Phil adds.

Joss had visited Kentmere Reservoir previously, while competing in a two-day mountain marathon. The runners had stopped overnight close to the reservoir and had been besieged by midges. 'They were savage; just like they are in Scotland,' he says, wincing with the memory of the bites. The midges hadn't yet appeared on the LMW though, and Joss was still enjoying his run. 'It'd been nice, easy running up the valley. It wasn't hard at all on the legs. I ran it very relaxed, like.' Joss had a little 'lie down' on the dam. 'Just closed my eyes for 10 minutes, didn't sleep though. It was grassy there, just like a good bed – nice, like – but I had to give missel a good shake to get on.' From there, his revised route took him over Nan Bield Pass before dropping towards Haweswater. 'I had a good run up there. I shortened me stride and got me legs used to climbing again. I ran well all that next section. I didn't really have a bad spell anywhere that day.'

But where would he have gone next if he'd had to drop back into Kentmere after visiting Haweswater, as originally planned? 'I was gonna go back out, and down till Hayeswater,' he says, indicating the steep, pathless headwall some way to the west of the main route out of the valley via Nan Bield.

'Just straight up?' asks Pete, incredulously. Let's remember, of course, that Joss would now have been running for 13 or 14 hours.

'Aye,' he says in a matter-of-fact tone. There's general laughter.

'As you would do...but only if you're Joss Naylor!' suggests Stephen.

'But I think the way I did it in the end was right,' adds Joss, seemingly oblivious to the wide eyes surrounding him.

Hemmed in by rocky slopes and sitting at just over 2000ft (640m) above sea level, Nan Bield Pass is one of the highest of the traditional routes through the eastern Lake District fells. It's home to a sturdy little shelter, the sort of place where fell-walkers will stop, get their sandwiches out, maybe a flask of coffee, and delight in the sense of being totally immersed in the mountains. For Joss though, it meant only another change of gear as he moved suddenly from uphill to downhill mode. On this perfect day, there was little difference between floating the downhill sections, flying the uphills or gliding effortlessly along the valley bottoms. With feet programmed, by decades on the fells, to

▲ Joss points out the route he took up to Nan Bield Pass

Nearing the head of the valley, the fells begin crowding in around us again

negotiate rocks and boulders almost unthinkingly, the steep descent to Small Water proved no problem at all.

Dave Elliott, who had parked up at Hartsop and climbed on to High Street with some of the apprentices, remembers the moment they spotted Joss and Alan Jackman far below. 'From this vantage point, we eventually saw them travelling from Small Water to Blea Water. We were in awe of Joss and how well he was covering the ground...and then to descend to Haweswater before coming all the way back up and over High Street...!'

From the dramatically located corrie tarn of Small Water, Joss headed north, over pathless ground, maintaining height. As the ground ahead dropped to the morass that is Mardale Waters

– where the water gathers, waiting for the moment when it's strong enough to begin its downhill journey to Haweswater – Joss swung west, over a grassy gap in a nose of rock and then along a rough ledge at the foot of remote, little-visited crags. After crossing one final spur – the line of grass-covered moraine that forms the tapering end of Mardale Ill Bell's northern ridge – he reached Blea Water and the path down to Haweswater.

The tricky bit had been finding that ideal line between Small Water and Blea Water, each occupying separate corries that glaciers had gouged out of the eastern face of the High Street range. Although Small Water was visited first, Blea Water is at a higher altitude. As always, it was important not to lose any height unnecessarily – and, if that meant venturing into remote, rugged terrain, so be it. Even after just a few outings on the fells with Joss, I realise his ability to find the perfect route is uncanny, almost second nature. 'The line was right coming through here,' he says, looking up at Piot Crag, part of the ridge that separates the two corries. 'I got the contours right that day. It was spot-on running – very remote, good, felly ground.' We don't take any chances on our rewalking of the route though. After visiting Small Water, enclosed by cloud-smothered fells, we drop to the edge of Mardale Waters and then have to climb back up to Blea Water. On paper at least, it's the long way round – and longer still for Pete who volunteers to climb back up to Small Water when Joss realises he's left his day-pack there – but it's safer.

> We're treated to one of those magical fell moments that linger long

Exquisitely poised on the lip of the corrie that bites into the fellside, Blea Water is Lakeland's deepest tarn. Although its outlet has been dammed to regulate the flow of water into the massive Haweswater Reservoir below, it is a natural feature and the construction of the dam made only a small impact on its maximum depth of 207ft (63m).

Standing at the water's edge, we're treated to one of those magical fell moments that linger long, if not forever, in the memories of walkers and runners – indeed of hill-goers of all varieties. While the crest of the high ground to our north is in brilliant sunshine, cloud pours over the crags to the south, filling the bowl below. There'd been a bank of low, stationary cloud over Small Water's corrie, but nothing like this; this is a seething mass of moist air, rushing full pelt in the strong wind, creating a cauldron of swirling vapour. The far side of the tarn is invisible at first, but then the mist breaks up and the sun illuminates much of the back wall. Within seconds though, the cliff is obscured again. Banks of mist keep rolling in and out – like curtains being pulled back and forth, concealing and revealing and concealing again. It's the movement and the constant state of flux that is the most entrancing. Despite all our combined years of fell experience – well into triple figures – we stand mesmerised. Dragging ourselves away from the scene, down the trail that leads to Haweswater, is easier said than done.

▲ At Blea Water

▲ Kentmere Reservoir with Ill Bell towering over it

A TALE OF TWO RESERVOIRS

Because of its significant drop in height over a relatively short distance, the Kent is one of the fastest-flowing rivers in England, making it ideal for powering mills. In the 1840s, some of the mill owners along its banks came together and paid to have its upper reaches dammed so that the flow could be regulated, the result being Kentmere Reservoir. The river continued to serve the mills for more than 100 years, the last factory to use its power being the James Cropper paper mill in the early 1970s. There was talk, in the 1990s, of demolishing the dam after it was found to be structurally unsound. After protests though, James Cropper plc, the de facto owner, paid to have it repaired.

With a surface area of less than 40 acres (16 hectares), Kentmere is only a small reservoir – unlike its massive neighbour on the other side of Nan Bield Pass…

Haweswater has a surface area of 964 acres (390 hectares) and can hold up to 18 billion gallons (82 billion litres) of water. (Kentmere Reservoir's 220 million gallons really is just a 'drop in the ocean' in comparison.) It was created in the first half of the 20th century when the growing population of Manchester, with its thirst unquenched by the creation of Thirlmere several decades earlier, set its sights on the eastern Lake District as a potential location for an even bigger reservoir project. An Act of Parliament was passed in 1919, allowing work to start on the enormous dam and giving the green light for the area's inhabitants to be moved. The people of two villages, Measand and Mardale Green, as well as several scattered farmsteads, had to be moved out of the valley, and almost 100 bodies that were buried in Holy Trinity churchyard had to be exhumed and reburied in Shap before the valley was flooded in 1935.

Since 1955, water has travelled from the Lake District along the Haweswater Aqueduct to a water treatment facility north of Manchester. This gravity-fed, underground pipeline, which took 22 years to build, is 67 miles (109km) long and now carries 125 million gallons (almost 570 million litres) of water per day. Having identified 'areas of concern' following a survey of the aqueduct in the early 21st century, water company United Utilities has announced it will be replacing all six tunnel sections by 2033 – a massive, multi-million-pound project that will take 10 years to complete.

STAGE 7

Start	Eastern end of Robin Lane, near Old Post Office, Troutbeck (NY 407 026)
Finish	Mardale Head car park, southern end of Haweswater (NY 469 107)
Distance	13.9 miles (22.4km)
Ascent	3450ft (1052m)
Approximate walking time	7–8hr

▶ With the Old Post Office café on your left, head north along the lane and immediately turn right. Just before the junction with the **A592**, cross the footbridge on the right. Follow the roadside path for 115 metres and then take the track climbing on the opposite side of the road. This heads south-south-east at first and later bends north-east to join up with the Longmire Road and then the **Garburn Road**.

▶ Eventually, the Garburn Road drops beside some cottages in **Kentmere** and on to Hollin Lane. Turn left and follow the lane past the church. Take the next surfaced lane on the left and, in 120 metres, climb the steps on the right to join a path heading uphill. Emerging on a lane in the part of Kentmere known as **Green Quarter** (below Green Quarter Fell), go left and, almost immediately, through a gate on the right to join a bridleway. (Return to this point after visiting Skeggles Water.) The bridleway winds its way on to open fell – roughly south at first but then swinging north-east.

▶ Just after a ruin to the right of the track, you reach a junction with another bridleway. Go straight across – on the less well-used path. This makes its way down to **Skeggles Water**, but disappears before reaching the water's edge. From the tarn, retrace your steps to the lane in **Green Quarter**, and turn right. Ignore one lane up to the right and then a road dropping left. About 275 metres beyond this second junction though, take the path dropping left. This valley-bottom route leads all the way to Kentmere Reservoir; simply keep left at all junctions until you go through the farm gate to the right of the large barn at **Tongue House**. At this point, the route heads right, along the south-west flank of Tongue Scar, to reach **Kentmere Reservoir**. From the north-east end of the dam, climb north-east. After about 0.5 miles (800 metres) of pathless ascent, you'll reach the bridleway. Turn left along this.

▲ A restricted byway links Troutbeck with Kentmere

▶ From the shelter at **Nan Bield Pass**, descend north to **Small Water** and cross the tarn's outlet stream. Follow the path as it drops into the valley, where it joins a broader track to reach the Mardale Head car park at the road-end, near the shores of **Haweswater**. (The route to Blea Water is described in Stage 8. Although on his 1983 run Joss visited both Small Water and Blea Water before dropping down to Haweswater, the route described in this book descends from Small Water to Haweswater then climbs back up to Blea Water.)

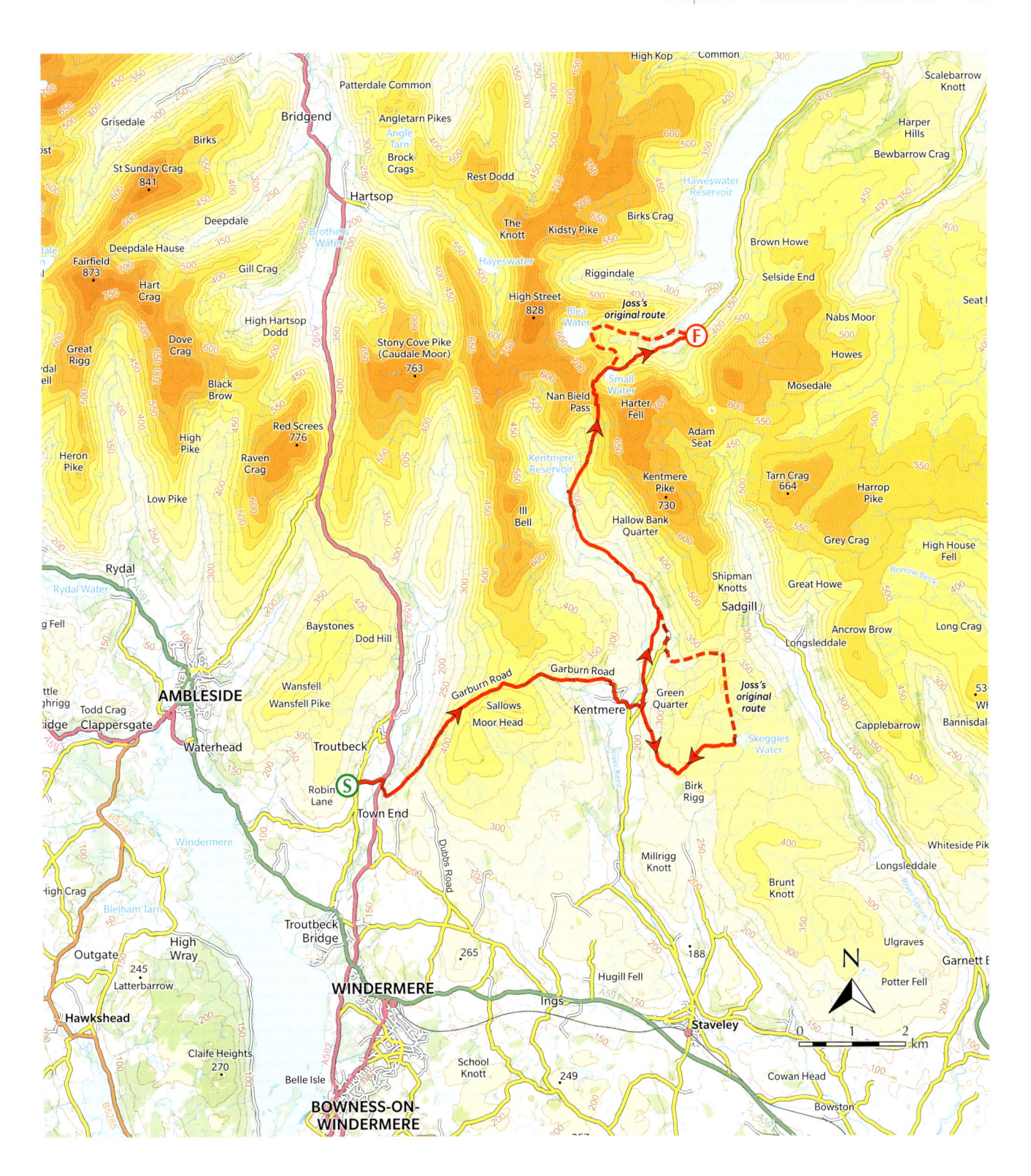

Chapter 7 – Troutbeck to Haweswater 107

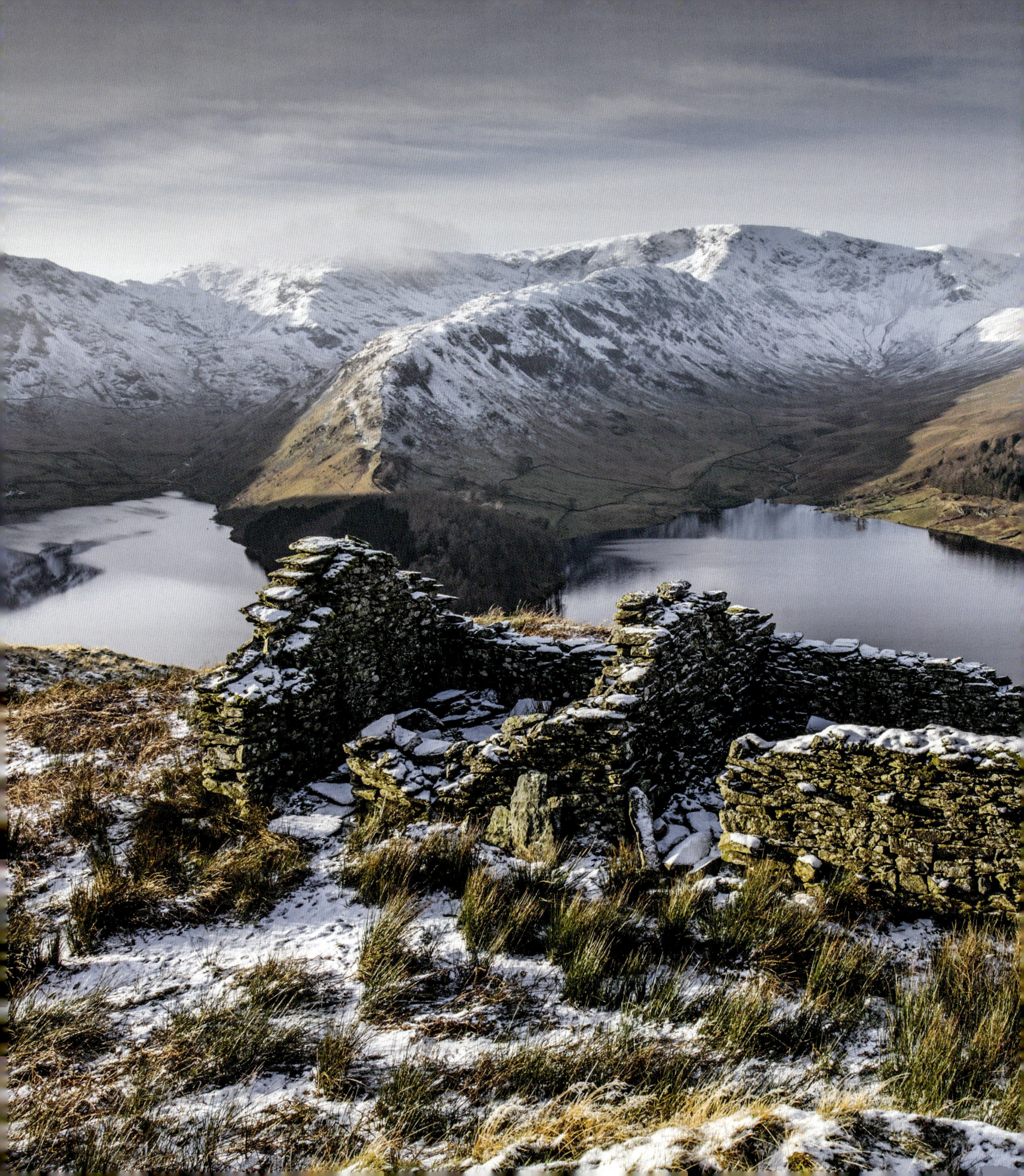

CHAPTER 8
Haweswater to Glenridding
(Haweswater, Hayeswater, Brothers Water, Ullswater)

It was 17:56 when Joss was greeted at the shores of Haweswater by his usual support team plus one of Dave Elliott's marshals. He was now an hour and 24 minutes ahead of schedule and, despite having covered 72 miles since leaving Loweswater in the early hours of the morning, there was no sign of him tiring or slowing down. He sat on a grassy ledge with his back to the wall, sipped a drink, had a bite of one of his wife Mary's rock buns and was off again.

His route took him over The Rigg, the low, eastern tip of the ridge that most other LMW runners would join after visiting Blea Water, and into Riggindale. This remote valley is enclosed by Kidsty Pike to the north and the dark cliffs of Riggindale Crag and Rough Crag to the south. 'I ran the valley bottom and went straight up to the skyline,' he recalls, pointing to the Straits of Riggindale, the narrow band of high ground that links these two rocky walls. After a hot, sunny day, the heat by the reservoir shores and in the valley bottom was oppressive. There was barely a breath of breeze to ruffle the water's surface. As Joss neared the dale head though, the lengthening shadows thrown out by High Street to the west provided some relief.

The sight of red deer in the Lake District remains a moment to be savoured

Like much of the ground between Haweswater and Ullswater, Riggindale is frequented by red deer. Unlike in the Scottish Highlands where their numbers are extremely high and hill-goers are used to seeing them, the sight of red deer in the Lake District remains a moment to be savoured. The animals that roam these fells are thought to be part of England's oldest native herd of red deer, the only ones that haven't cross-bred with sika deer, introduced from eastern Asia in the 19th century. The ancient deer forest itself is centred on The Nab, the solitary fell that splits the head of

▲ A quick drink and he'll be on his way again (Photo credit: Dave Elliott)

◀ Haweswater from the old corpse road

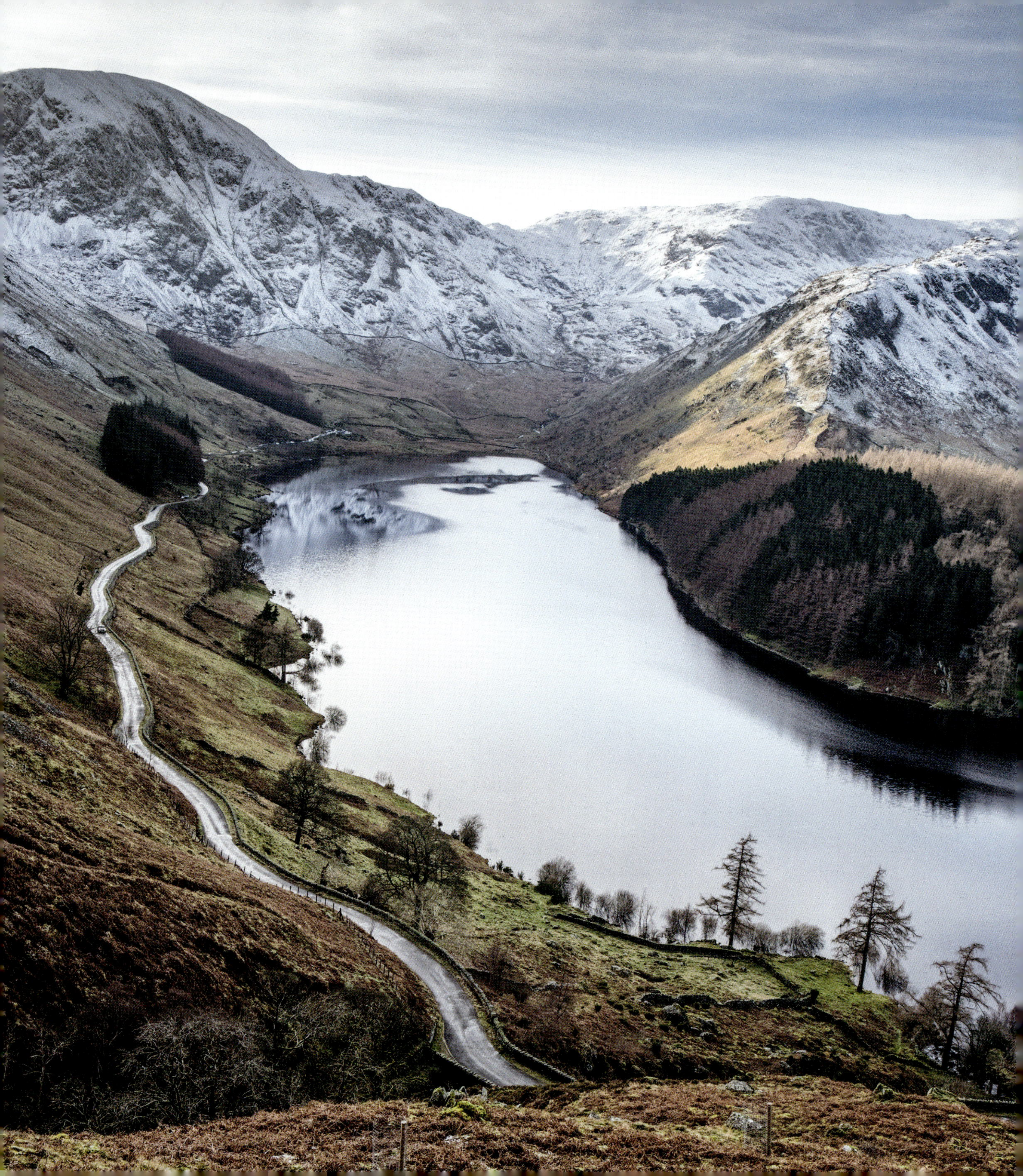

Martindale in two, but the deer frequently range into neighbouring Mardale and Kentmere, and can often be seen grazing near the head of Riggindale. The high number of deer in the area historically is reflected in several local place names, including the hamlet Hartsop, meaning 'valley of the hart', Harter Fell and Hart Crag.

Joss doesn't remember seeing any red deer on his LMW run, and neither does he recall seeing the golden eagles that lived in the valley at the time. He'd seen the massive birds of prey on other visits to the area though and in Blengdale in the western Lakes. He says there were golden eagles in this remote Wasdale side valley until the early 1980s. 'It's a shame they got shot out,' he adds. 'These pheasant men don't like eagles.' He also remembers a time when ptarmigan would put in an appearance in the Lake District, including a breeding pair on Haycock, and small flocks on Bow Fell and Kirk Fell.

It's a punishingly steep climb up the dale head, and Joss was careful to avoid any of the crags that project from it. After reaching the grassy ground on the fell top – where legionaries once marched along the highest Roman road in the country – he began his descent to Hayeswater. 'I come down t' dry gill there,' he says as we later stand beside the motionless body of water, enjoying the serenity of this elongated bowl between High Street and Gray Crag. He points to a gully leading down to the southern end of the tarn but then hesitates as he takes his mind back 37 years, picturing his route. 'I'm sure I did. We came across the straits of High Street from Riggindale. I found a good drop-in place – didn't need to check much – and we came in at t' top end. I didn't realise there was so much lake ahead of us though.' Running the eastern shoreline, made hummocky by the mounds of moraine deposited here by glacial ice, slowed him down. 'That was my biggest mistake, like.'

Back then, Joss would've crossed Hayeswater Gill near the dam, but today we cross via the 'new' footbridge a few

> Where legionaries once marched along the highest Roman road in the country

◀ Haweswater and Mardale Head

▲ Winter's afternoon at Hayeswater

hundred yards downstream. The natural tarn had been dammed in 1908 to provide water for local communities, but its role as a reservoir came to an end in the early part of the 21st century, its dam and neighbouring bridge being dismantled by the water company United Utilities in 2014.

As we head downstream, the tranquillity of the tarn is replaced by the roar of the beck as it comes thundering over a series of small waterfalls and down smooth rock chutes. We have to raise our voices to be heard over the tumult. 'I knocked it out of gear coming down here,' shouts Joss, remembering how he flew down from the reservoir. On the far side of the beck, the old filter house has been restored, and awaits the green light for reincarnation as a holiday cottage. Further down the gill sits a ruined stone barn, its roof thick with greenery – a layer of ferns and mosses several inches deep, an unseemly hairpiece.

Beyond the barn, the sharp nose of Raven Crag protrudes from the eastern slopes of Hartsop Dodd, hanging out over the side

▶ Joss and Alan Jackman descending towards Hayeswater in 1983 (Photo credit: Dave Elliott)

▼ Ruined barn, Hayeswater Gill

valley of Pasture Beck. As the name suggests, ravens nest here most summers, building a home of twigs, soil and moss, lined with softer materials such as grass and wool. Pairs mate for life – 'life' meaning up to 15 years for birds in the wild – and will stay in the same area all that time, defending their territory aggressively.

Joss recalls a time, on Scoat Fell, when he saw dozens of these impressive birds, the largest member of the crow family, feasting on a massive swarm of insects that looked like crane flies. 'You don't normally see ravens in such big groups – there's normally just one or two of them – but I counted 55, and they were there for 10 days. I've never seen that quantity of ravens together since.' Lost in his memories, he continues: 'There was this one time I was coming over the top of Black Sail, and it was just turning dusk, and there were these two ravens. The only thing you could hear was their wings cutting the air – it was such an eerie noise.'

Hartsop would once have been a hive of industrial activity

The area around Hartsop would once have been a hive of industrial activity. There were two lead mines nearby as well as a large slate quarry on Caudale Moor. We spot the scant remains of Myers Head mine as we come down the track beside Hayeswater Gill. Close to where Pasture Beck enters the gill is a wheel pit, which would once have housed the huge water wheel constructed to drain the flood-prone mine. Just above this are the stone piers that supported the wooden channel used for diverting water from Hayeswater Gill to turn the wheel. This operated until the mine was abandoned in the 1870s.

As we reach the sheepfolds on the edge of the hamlet of Hartsop, a few strands of wool cling to fences, where the ewes have been brushing up against them. More telling are the small pieces of fleece still lying around on the ground – evidence that the sheep, mostly Swaledales and Herdwicks, have recently been gathered for their annual shearing. We've probably only missed the spectacle by days. They'll be back out on the fells now, looking rather pitiful after the removal of their weighty coats.

When Joss was at Bowderdale, he kept Herdwicks (with a few Swaledales for cross-breeding), shearing more than 2000 every year. 'Once, I could clip loads in a day with a pair of hand shears. One of me brothers, he was a really good clipper, and he could do even more. There was this one day – we started about six in the morning, and just kept going – and we clipped about 300. But you weren't to hang about.' It was hard graft, made harder by the back problems that have plagued Joss since childhood. 'I've had

▲ Joss kept Herdwicks when he farmed at Bowderdale

▶ A young Joss clipping at Bowderdale (Photo from Joss's own collection; photographer unknown)

two or three really bad knock-ups,' he says, referring to the times when he's been incapacitated for days. 'There was this once where I hadn't walked for practically a fortnight – I was lying with two or three pillows under me stomach, living on painkillers. But I had to go and gather me sheep; I had 2000 to shear. I was in that much pain when I was clipping, sweat was running down me legs; I had a towel tied round me waist. It was bloody agony.'

The price hill farmers get for their fleeces today is relatively low, but there is evidence in Hartsop of a time when wool was big business in the Lake District. Many of the cottages that line the hamlet's single, narrow lane today, some dating from the 17th century,

▲ A moody autumn day at Brothers Water

Chapter 8 – Haweswater to Glenridding   115

still have external spinning galleries. Located on the first floor of the homes, tucked under the eaves, this is where the women of the house would have carded the wool (to disentangle, clean and align the fibres) and then spun it. This would have been done both for domestic use and as part of a wider cottage industry involving fellmongers, weavers, fullers and various packmen.

As the sun lowered in the sky and Joss passed through Hartsop, a man ran out into the lane from one of these slate cottages with an unusual offer for the long-distance runner. 'I've got a bath waiting for you inside if you wanna come in…' This was Ed Hill, who used to run mountain marathons with the Lancashire fell-running legend George Brass. He'd only recently moved to Hartsop from Clitheroe but had heard about Joss's LMW attempt and wanted to help in some way. Still some time ahead of schedule, Joss barely hesitated. 'I went in, stripped off and jumped in this bath. He had everything set up for us. It freshened us up, like, especially me feet – they hadn't had a good cool off since I stood in Windermere. I didn't hang around though; I was off again pretty quick, like.'

> 'Got a bath waiting for you inside if you wanna come in…'

'Off again', down through Hartsop, over a footbridge spanning Pasture Beck and out along an enclosed path to the main road. Crossing over, he 'was pretty quick' too about his encounter with Brothers Water – just dipping his hand in and barely registering its surroundings. On the tranquil morning when we visit the valley-bottom lake in 2020 though, he lingers longer, enjoying the scenery and posing for photographs with Pete Todhunter's son, Ryan, who has joined us for the day, fresh from his training as a rower with the prestigious Leander Club on the Thames in Berkshire. Joss is laughing at something Ryan has said, and the laughter lingers on his face and in his eyes as he looks, silently now, across the lake to where the sharp nose of High Hartsop Dodd seems to dive almost to the water's edge. Directly opposite, dense woodland reaches surprisingly high into the glorious side valley of Dovedale while, below the woods, two swans glide gracefully across the trees' reflection. 'It's summat special, in't it?' says Joss.

Brothers Water used to be known as Broad Water. The local story is that its name was changed in the 19th century after two brothers drowned there. Its outlet stream, Goldrill Beck, flows north, reaching the southern tip of Ullswater after a couple of gently meandering miles. Joss ran the road in 1983, keeping to the western side of the valley, but there is also a decent track that heads downstream along the eastern side of the beck. Hill farmers make the most of this relatively fertile valley bottom, using the fields largely for winter grazing and to grow some fodder crops, but their options are limited as the flat ground quickly gives way to fell. The valley really only broadens out north of Patterdale, too late for the farmers and their livestock though as the level ground is already occupied... by the Lake District's second largest body of water.

Serpentine in nature, Ullswater snakes its way for eight miles from the rolling farmland and low moorland at Pooley Bridge, at its north-eastern end, to Glenridding and Patterdale, where the fells crowd in, crags tumbling right down to the water's edge in places. Few lakes are accompanied by such a striking and alluring change of scenery over their length. Like Wastwater, Joss's home lake, Ullswater is fed by becks that come hurtling down from some of England's highest mountains – in this case, the fells of the mighty Helvellyn range. The water ends up in the River Eden, the longest river solely within Cumbria, discharged into the Irish Sea via the Solway Firth on England's border with Scotland.

We stroll down to the water's edge close to St Patrick's Boat Landing, Joss whistling something from his seemingly endless

Ullswater is fed by becks that come hurtling down from some of England's highest mountains

repertoire along the way. (I've given up trying to 'name that tune' but the melodies always sound half-familiar, a conglomeration of various songs. Just when I think I've identified it, it morphs into something else. When quizzed, Joss always says he makes them up as he goes along.) Day-packs are deposited on the beach as he again poses for photographs under the hot sun.

It was just past eight in the evening – a muggy evening – when Joss reached the lake in 1983. Stopping for an impromptu bath in Hartsop had done little to dent his time, and he was still 52 minutes ahead of schedule. 'We touched the water, had a la'al stop in Glenridding for five minutes to refuel, and then it was up to Sticks Pass.' He looks up in the direction of the high fells. He clearly loves the valleys, loves standing beside lakes looking up, wandering along old bridleways and exploring ancient woods, but the admiration and respect in his eyes – and that slight sense of longing – tells us where he'd always rather be.

▲ It was late evening by the time Joss reached Ullswater (Photo credit: Dave Elliott)

▲ Ullswater, Lakeland's second largest lake

ALEX'S STORY

When he was a teenager, Alex Smith knew Joss only as a local legend; he remembers going out to watch him pass through Bootle, where Alex grew up, on a charity run. As a fellow member of the Cumberland Fell Runners, Alex was honoured to accompany the great man on some of the final miles of his LMW attempt. 'Fresh' from the Blake Fell Race earlier in the day, which he'd completed in 53min 18sec, he met Joss at Brothers Water and continued with him for much of the rest of the route. The following is taken from an article he wrote about the experience for the January 1984 edition of *The Fell Runner*, the magazine of the Fell Runners Association:

'It was at Brothers Water that I met Joss, 80 miles down the road, almost exactly an hour ahead of schedule and as bright as a button. After a brief stop, we set off down the road towards Ullswater, Joss shirtless in the warm evening, enquiring about the results of the Blake Fell Race and making light of his day's exertions.

'At Ullswater one of the support crew produced a copy of *The Times* which featured a photograph and an article about "the flying shepherd". "They must be pretty short of news," was Joss's curt verdict. If I'd taken the trouble to read the article...I would have seen that "Joss rates this run as only medium hard" which might have made a good conversational gambit later in the day.

'From Ullswater we ran the last fell section – through Glenridding, over Sticks Pass and down to Thirlmere where we were greeted by the worst midges of the summer. I sheltered in a support car, but Joss braved the outside world which may explain why it was such a short break.

'From there, the route lay along the road and over fields to Derwentwater. Despite it being virtually the longest day, the sky clouded over at sunset and darkness set in quickly...A group of apprentices from British Nuclear Fuels Ltd had sorted out the shortest route to the lake which involved a scramble across fields, along darkened footpaths and through a small forest in the gathering gloom before finally arriving at the lakeshore in near darkness. Here, Joss stopped for the famous Naylor shake – to get his legs "loosed off" – and a brief towel down. My legs feeling shaky enough already, I just stopped for some of Mary's fruitcake which I can certainly recommend to any other aspiring Lakes, Meres and Waters runners.'

STAGE 8

Start Mardale Head car park, southern end of Haweswater (NY 469 107)

Finish Bridge over Glenridding Beck on A592, Glenridding (NY 386 169)

Distance 9.4 miles (15.1km)

Ascent 2470ft (753m)

Approximate walking time 5hr–5hr 30min

▸ Take the path beyond the gates at the road-end. When it splits in three, turn right. After the bridge over Mardale Beck, go left. From **Blea Water**, follow a faint trail climbing north-west. On joining the ridge, follow the clearer path west, ascending **Long Stile**. As soon as the gradient relents, head north along the eastern rim of **High Street**'s grassy plateau. A wall, to the left, soon acts as a guide. Follow the path around the northern side of **The Knott** and then bear left at a faint fork to drop to the northern end of **Hayeswater**. Follow the outlet stream for a short while and cross via the footbridge. Turn right along the clear track, descending to **Hartsop**.

▸ About 210 metres beyond the car park on the eastern edge of the hamlet, bear left to pass between two stone buildings and cross **Pasture Beck**. Follow the path south-west to the **A592**. Cross diagonally left, through a small gate, and head down to the edge of **Brothers Water**. Retrace your steps to the road and turn left. Take the next road on the right, as if heading back to **Hartsop**, but then turn left – beside the white house. Beyond the entrance to Hartsop Fold, the lane becomes a rough track. Continue north along the valley bottom, passing the buildings at **Beckstones** and **Crookabeck**.

▸ Go left at a junction of lanes and then turn right at the main road. Using a series of roadside paths, follow the **A592** through **Patterdale** and into **Glenridding**. The shores of **Ullswater** can be accessed via the small gate just after the entrance to the car park at St Patrick's Boat Landing. The road bridge over **Glenridding Beck** is 245 metres north of this.

▲ Hayeswater Gill

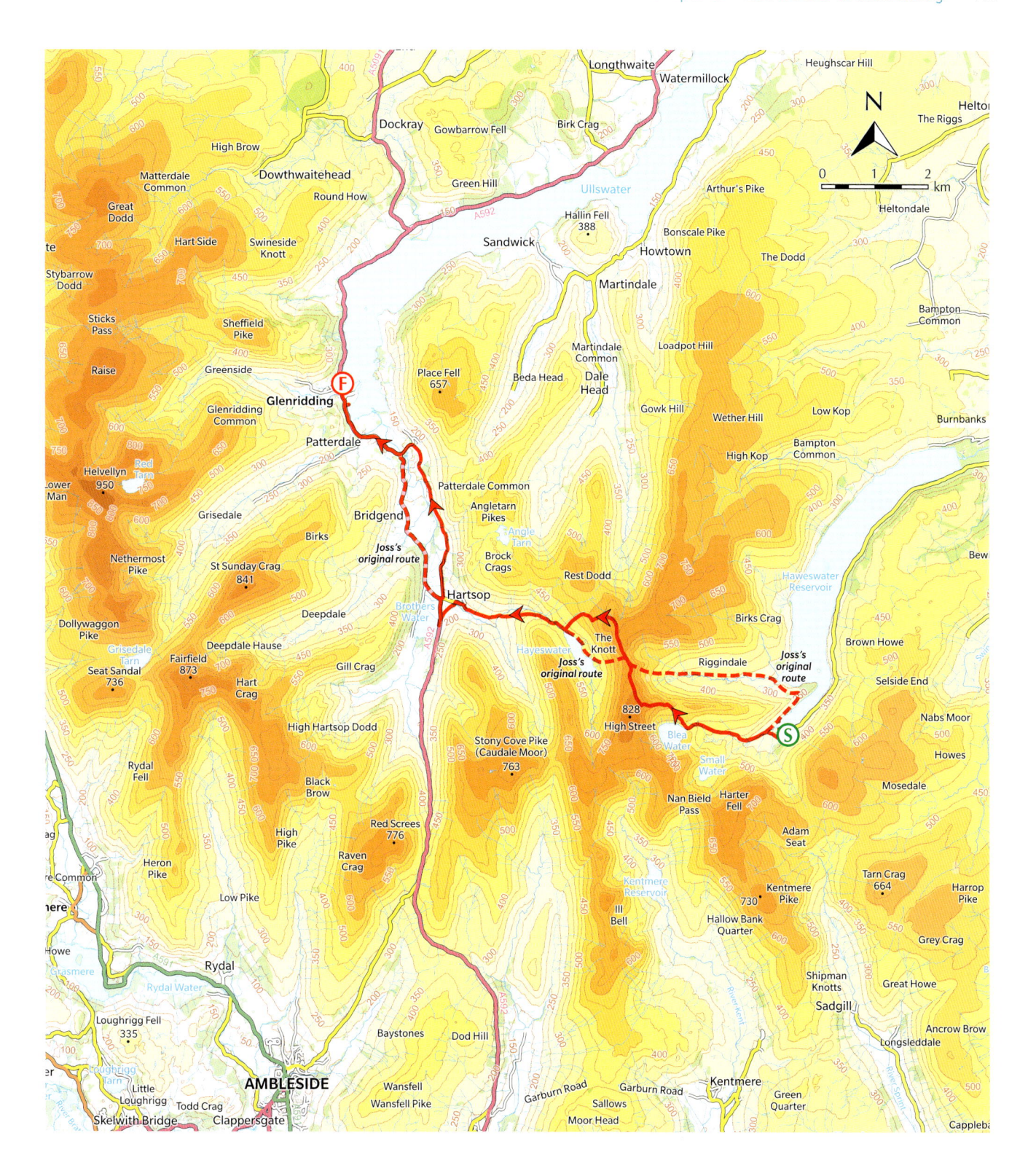

Chapter 8 – Haweswater to Glenridding   119

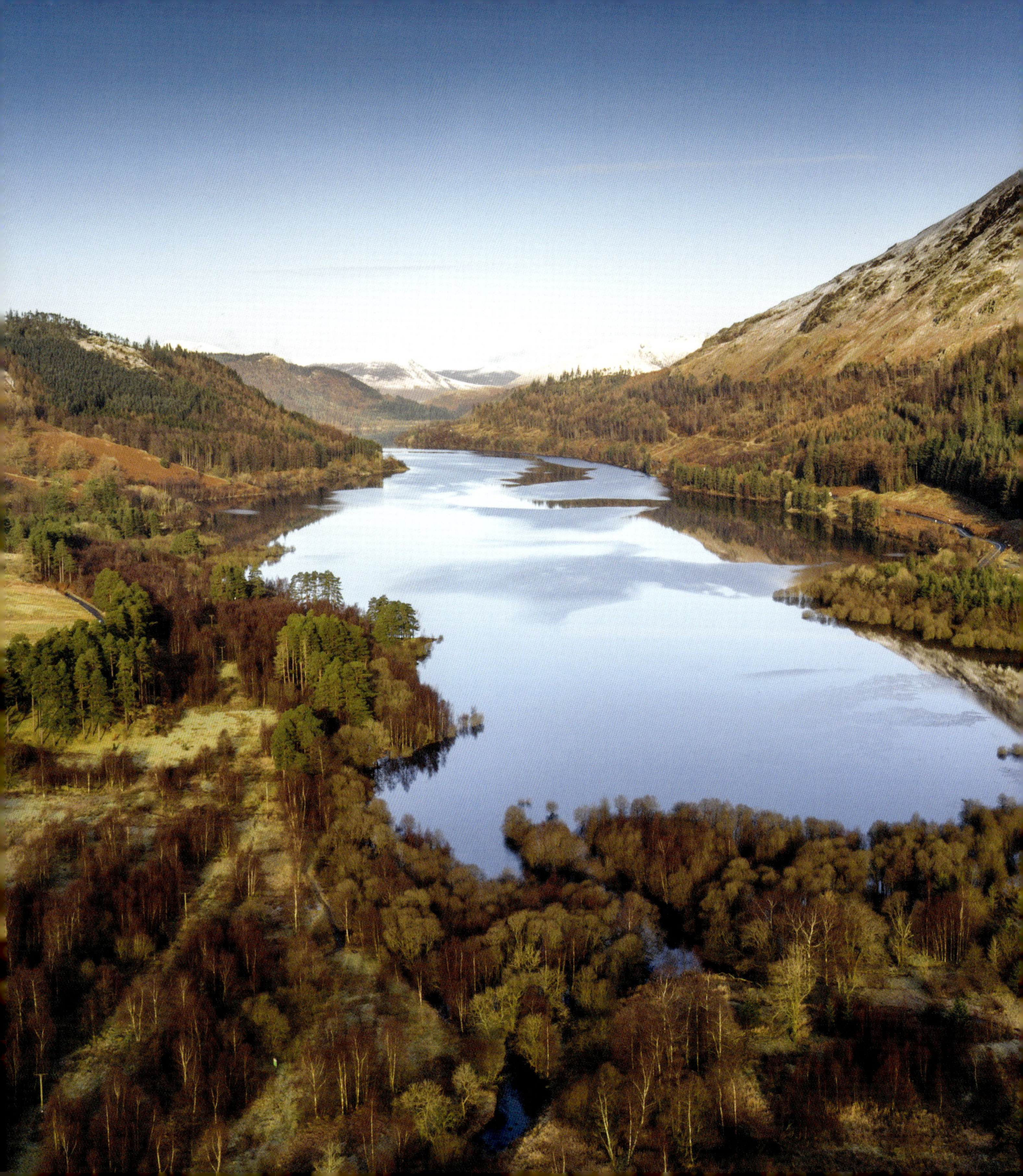

CHAPTER 9
Glenridding to Keswick
(Thirlmere)

As he left Glenridding, Joss edged ever closer to breaking the LMW record of 25hr 16min set by Alan Heaton the previous summer, but he took nothing for granted. He still had about 24 miles left – nearly a whole marathon – and that was after having already run more than 80 miles – or more than three marathons. And let's not forget about all those fells he'd climbed along the way. After all, his tired body would be remembering them very clearly by this point in the day.

The rush of Glenridding Beck mirrored his continuing momentum as he bounded up the valley, but while the beck benefitted from gravity, Joss was heading in the opposite direction.

The power of the beck, which begins life on Helvellyn, is evident throughout the valley. Its channel is littered with enormous boulders, chunks of bedrock that have been ripped from the ground by the water's force and then deposited downstream. This is the beck that, during the storms of December 2015, repeatedly flooded Glenridding, leaving business owners and householders in despair as they cleaned away the debris left by one deluge only to face the same situation days later. On the other hand, this is also the beck that has had its tremendous power harnessed in the past for

▲ From left, Alan Jackman, Dave Elliott and Joss near Ullswater
(Photo credit: Dave Elliott)

◀ Thirlmere

▲ Ullswater

▲ Sticks Pass this way

the good of the area, its water being used by the Greenside mine. In fact, Greenside, once the largest lead mine in England, was the first in Britain to use electrical winding gear and underground haulage, all of which were powered by water turbines.

Beyond the former buildings of the Greenside mine – one, a miners' hostel, now converted to YHA accommodation – Joss was able to look up into the higher reaches of Glenridding Beck. The north face of Catstye Cam, almost perpetually in shadow, loomed dark over its southern banks. Joss's route, though, now took him out of the valley and up towards Sticks Pass. A rough path leads up through the juniper that still grows on the steep fellside here and into a landscape made desolate by mining. After the beautiful, bucolic Ullswater valley, this was a lot more austere, a reminder of Lakeland's history, of the mining that ripped into the heart of the fells for centuries. Even today, nothing grows on the spoil heaps beside Swart Beck – hardly surprising given the toxicity of the minerals worked here. Enormous holes in the fellside, marked incorrectly on OS maps as disused quarries, are where mine workings have collapsed in on themselves.

'It's bleak, in't it? There's no appeal to it,' says Joss. 'You go by and you can't help but wonder what happened here. You start to think about them old lads coming up and working in them mines, and they'd be working hard all day. They'd have very little heat. It would've been like working in rabbit holes – some of them little seams – sometimes just with candles. It doesn't bear thinking about. They'd be doing a lot of splitting with wedges and sledgehammers. And then, when they got a bit out, they'd get an old bogie with iron wheels and an old horse or pony to pull it.'

There would also have been dozens of surface workers, mostly women and children in the early days of the mine, smashing up the rocks by hand and sifting through the noxious material. Like the mining itself, this would have been a very demanding process and a poisonous one at that, leading to abdominal problems, learning difficulties in children, memory loss, kidney disease, high blood pressure, reproductive issues and problems relating to the central nervous system. 'Most people today don't realise what went on in these places,' Joss adds. 'But they must've had a hard life – just an existence, all graft and little more, because they'd be working for pennies.'

Beyond the scars of Greenside, the route heads up Sticks Gill to the top of the pass – at 2444ft (745m) above sea level, one of the highest points on the entire LMW route and a moment of sudden change. For Joss, all was new again. The confines of the gill disappeared, and the col lifted him into another land, providing a fresh perspective. The view, the landscape, the geology, the light – they were all altered by one single footstep that brought him to this place.

Located part way between Raise and Stybarrow Dodd, the top of Sticks Pass forms part of a long ridge that Helvellyn throws out to the north. Never dropping below 2000ft for more than seven glorious miles, it forms one of the best stretches of sustained high-level walking or running in the whole of the Lake District. On his LMW run though, Joss's experience of the ridge lasted just seconds; from the pass, he was off down the other side again, his final taste of the high ground on this momentous day. In our rewalking of it, we do at least rest at the top, lying back on the grass and moss to consider these last few miles – watched all the while by a solitary Herdwick ewe, chewing. It's the most relaxed I've seen Joss while stationary; usually, he's itching to get going as soon as we've eaten. I get the impression that, if it weren't for the rest of us wanting to stop for a while, he would probably eat on the hoof, or at least standing up. Today though, after he's offered his ever-present box of biscuits around, it doesn't immediately go back into his day-pack.

Despite it being a slightly overcast day, the views to the east are good – we can see right across the Eden Valley to the North Pennines in the distance. Joss points out the route of the 1962 Mountain Trial, the one he and all but one of the other runners had to retire from. It took in part of this ridge and the Helvellyn range, as well as High Street on the other side of the main valley and Place Fell. 'Weather was bloody bad all the time,' he says, recalling the wind and the cold rain that fell throughout the September event. The ewe continues her ruminating, unimpressed; she's seen worse conditions up here. Not surprising really, as we're less than an hour's walk from the top of Helvellyn, which experiences some of the harshest weather in the Lakes, particularly in winter when it's pummelled by blizzard after blizzard, and massive cornices form all along its eastern rim.

'A hard life – just an existence, all graft and little more'

▲ A moment's rest

▲ On the descent from Sticks Pass

'And then there was that time I did the Four Threes...What a day that was! Talk about rain!' Joss's memory has made another leap and he is now referring to the time, in 1975, when he ran the four Lake District 3000ft peaks – Skiddaw, Scafell, Scafell Pike and Helvellyn – as part of his training for another attempt on the 24-Hour Fell Record. He'd completed the Ramblers' Association's Lake District Four 3000ft Peaks Marathon Walk in 8hr 24min in June 1970 but was now hoping to run the gruelling 45-mile (72km) route in less than seven hours. He managed it in 7hr 29min, despite the weather and despite the fact that he was running in shoes that were two sizes too big for him. 'I lost them nine times coming down bloody Wythburn! They were a step up, though, from those Jesus sandals I saw someone wearing in a race once, with just a strap between the toes to keep them on. Bloody weirdo!'

'Let him go and he doesn't stop, a perpetual motion machine!'

Pete points out Hayeswater to the south-east, the 21st body of water on the LMW. It's hard to make out at first, but then the sun breaks through, briefly illuminating its surface so that it shines, beacon-like, in its bowl on the otherwise grey fells. 'That's a long way to come, Joss, from there to here,' he says. He goes quiet for a bit, doing the maths, and then, incredulous, adds: 'Bloody hell! It must be about nine miles, and all that climb in...what? just over an hour?' The ewe remains nonchalant; Joss barely responds. It's just what he did in those days. He ran. And he ran. And he ran.

When we finally tear ourselves away from the top, bidding farewell to the still resting ewe, and begin heading down the western side of the pass, Joss is moving so fast that his shortest companion (that's me) is practically having to run to keep up with him. Stephen likens him to a Slinky toy. 'Let him go and he doesn't stop,

Skiddaw, England's fourth highest mountain, can be seen behind Joss ▶

a perpetual motion machine!' When I catch him up, I ask about the secret to running downhill. He explains you need your knees slightly bent and, for racing at least, you have to take long strides. 'You just let your feet drop and get the tension out of your legs. It's like changing gear.' The oft-repeated mantra of fell-runners preparing for a speedy descent is 'brakes off, brain off'. It seems, if you want to win races, you've got to have confidence on the downhills, an ability simply to accept that hurtling down a scree path or a boulder-strewn slope won't end in disaster. (Well, that's the theory, at least.) I ask Joss if he was better at downhill or uphill. Without hesitation, he says he was good at both. There's no boasting; it's just a fact.

We enjoy a 'grand skyline' on our descent – Bow Fell and Great Gable are among the most prominent central peaks; to the west, Grisedale Pike and Dale Head stand out; but Skiddaw, just a few miles to the north-west, is the fell that dominates. A wisp of cloud occasionally tickles the summit. Each time I look up, the conditions on this hulking beast of a mountain have changed: cloud-free, cloud-covered, cloud-free, cloud-covered...A few other tops have more substantial, rain-bearing cloud on them. We're aware of a tiny bit of moisture in the cool wind, but it never amounts to much.

'There wasn't much of a path here when I came through; it was a grassy run in,' says Joss as we descend the bridleway. The going is generally good underfoot but there are sections that have been washed out. 'They can't cope with the tropical rain we get. Once water's started flowing down places like this, there's nowhere for it to go but the path. It needs drains cutting across.' Like many people who have spent their

> Skiddaw is the fell that dominates. A wisp of cloud occasionally tickles the summit

lives in Cumbria – indeed in just about any part of western Britain – he thinks the climate has got wetter over the years. It's not that they didn't get torrential downpours when he was younger, he explains, it's just that they happen a lot more frequently these days.

Beyond a neat sheepfold, restored recently by a team of volunteers, Joss slows down to peer into the steep confines of Stanah Gill. He didn't have a chance to take in the scenery like this back in 1983, so he's surprised to discover just how impressive a ravine it is. There's a waterfall, small but powerful, that's briefly visible from our side of the gill, and a surprisingly large tree. 'That's well sheltered,' he says.

Suddenly, he spots a lone lamb in the bottom of the gill and is clearly concerned for its safety. I'm thankful that no one in the group has a rope on them. I'm sure that Joss knows his days of roping up and climbing down a rock face to rescue stranded sheep are behind him now, but you can never be sure; even at 84, he seems, at times, to be invincible. Thankfully, we soon spot the lamb's mother and Joss's worries – and mine – are allayed.

Joss dipped his hands, again, in Manchester's water supply

From Stanah, the tiny fellside settlement at the bottom of the pass, the route heads to Thirlmere, number 24 on the list of 27 lakes, meres and waters. Like Haweswater, Thirlmere was created to serve the needs of the growing population of Manchester. It started life as two small, natural lakes and was then dammed in 1894. With typical Victorian ingenuity, engineers devised an aqueduct system that relied on gravity – no pumps involved – to move the water almost 100 miles.

It was 21:35 when Joss dipped his hands, again, in Manchester's water supply. He had originally thought the reservoir was directly opposite Stanah, so it was frustrating when he realised he'd have to run along the A591 and then down a side lane to reach it. At this stage, every second counted. In his haste, with goat-like sure-footedness, he clambered down the side of the dam, touched the water, clambered back up again and was gone in seconds.

One of the marshals at Thirlmere, Nigel Alderson, clearly remembers the moment. 'Gareth Hughes and I had camped out the day before and looked at two potential routes towards Derwentwater – by road or over the top. We walked both and found the road quickest,' he says. 'But Joss had other ideas. He said over the top was the fastest route and, with that, off he went – still with a spring in his step even at this late stage.'

A young Joss prepares to rescue sheep stranded on a crag ▶
(Photo from Joss's own collection; photographer unknown)

Chapter 9 – Glenridding to Keswick 127

▲ The descent towards Thirlmere steepens

Sellafield instrument apprentice instructor Tom Bell, who had already acted as a marshal at Low Water and now joined the growing band of runners from Thirlmere, was also impressed by Joss's stamina. 'He seemed remarkably fresh considering how far he had run,' he says, although his colleague's amazing level of fitness didn't come as a surprise. 'There were a few of us that used to go for a run at lunchtime with Joss,' he adds, thinking back to the early 1980s at the nuclear plant. 'He generally talked non-stop while the rest of us were struggling to get a breath.'

Dave Elliott, who had been at every road stop and had even run a few short stretches with Joss throughout the day, also joined him on his way into Keswick. 'He'd been worried about taking a convoluted route into Keswick and asked if I could find a shorter way,' Dave recalls. 'Joss much preferred to be off the tarmac at this stage knowing that the rest of the run from Derwentwater was all road. So, I'd been out a few weeks earlier and found a route that took us down by the woods near Walla Crag. I joined him on that section. Not wanting to delay him, I set off at a good pace before he shouted, "Whoa! Whoa! I've got nearly a hundred miles in me legs! How about you?" I took the hint and slowed down.'

By now, the weather had changed. The beautiful sunset associated with many a Cumbrian midsummer evening had failed to materialise and the fells were draped in cloud. 'It just shut in all at once,' Joss recalls. When he reached the car park that was home to Century Theatre's 'Blue Box' – the set of leaky metal trailers that was the predecessor to today's Theatre by the Lake – there was a 'thin shower of drizzle'. This was to be his last rest of the day, and he spent 15 minutes with his support team. After a drink, a bite to eat and a quick rub down, he was off again. Off into the night...

> 'Whoa! Whoa! I've got nearly a hundred miles in me legs!'

THE MOUNTAIN TRIAL

The Lake District Mountain Trial, first run in 1952, was one of a new breed of amateur fell races, quite different from the early professional guides' races. It was started by the Lakeland Regional Group of the Youth Hostels Association as part of the organisation's 21st anniversary celebrations. Those early competitors had to be YHA members and, wearing boots or 'stout' shoes, they ran a course from the Old Dungeon Ghyll in Great Langdale to Scafell Pike, also taking in Bow Fell and Great Gable. This was a radical departure from the much shorter guides' races where runners, competing for cash prizes, would trail up and down a single fell from a valley base. Within a few years, an orienteering element was added to the Mountain Trial, making it the first race of its type in the country.

Joss first competed in a Mountain Trial in 1960 – his first ever competitive run, in fact. He turned up in his heavy work boots, with long trousers cut off at the knees. His first race win was at the 1966 trial, from the Woolpack Inn in Eskdale, when he completed the course in 4hr 18min 20sec. He won again in 1969, then every year from 1971 to 1977, and finally in 1979 – an unequalled 10 wins.

Joss competed in 54 Lake District Mountain Trials in total, running the 'short' course from 2007 onwards and as part of a team with his son-in-law Peter Ferris in later years. He failed to complete the 1962 event when atrocious weather forced him to retire at Red Tarn, the second checkpoint. This was a trial that went down in fell-running history, with some of the top competitors of the time, including Eric Beard, also defeated by the wind and rain. The only runner to finish was George Brass. Alan Heaton and some other competitors, realising that Joss was in difficulty, helped carry him part way down the fell but he quickly recovered and was able to continue the descent unaided. The incomplete course was always something that 'bothered him' so he finally finished it in 2019, at the age of 83, raising money for the Brathay Trust in the process.

▲ Joss sets off on the 1975 Mountain Trial at Seathwaite in Dunnerdale.
Also pictured are A Elliott (centre) and DJG Holmes (Photo from Joss's own collection; photographer unknown)

◀ Bassenthwaite Lake, number 26, beckons in the distance

STAGE 9

Start	Bridge over Glenridding Beck on A592, Glenridding (NY 386 169)
Finish	Derwentwater landing stages, Keswick (NY 264 227)
Distance	11.9 miles (19.2km)
Ascent	2500ft (762m)
Approximate walking time	6–7hr

▸ Head north along the **A592** and immediately turn left. Don't enter the car park though; instead, follow the loop road round to the right and then turn left along Greenside Road. Beyond the **Greenside** mine buildings, continue up the gravel zigzags and then bear right at a signposted fork – for Sticks Pass. A rough path winds its way up the fellside and then towards some spoil heaps. Soon after the bridge over Swart Beck, swing north-west through the barren landscape to pick up the path up Sticks Gill.

▸ At a crossing of routes at **Sticks Pass**, go straight over and descend towards **Stanah Gill**. Nearing the valley bottom, bear right to cross Sty Beck and then follow the path down to a lane. Turn left. Go left again at the road and then turn right along the **A591**. Take the next road on the left and follow it across **Thirlmere** dam. (A gate on the left just before the next road junction provides access to the reservoir's shores.) Take the next road on the right after the dam, and quickly turn right again.

▸ After 0.6 miles (1km) on this road, bear left along a track that continues skirting the base of the forest. In a further 0.5 miles (800 metres), bear right along a narrower path. Enter the yard at **Shoulthwaite Farm** and follow the access lane round to the right to reach the **A591**. Turn left and follow the busy road for 1.6 miles (2.6km), partly on pavement. Drawing level with Castle Lane and a bus stop, turn left through a gate. A clear path heads roughly south-west along field edges. When it ends, turn right through the gate and continue beside the wall on the right to reach a minor road. Turn left and, almost immediately, take the path to the right.

▸ Cross **Brockle Beck** and head downstream – ignoring both a footpath to the left and a bridge to the right – to reach a gate. Go through, past Springs Farm and on to a residential street on the edge of **Keswick**. About 455 metres beyond Springs Farm, turn left on to a narrow path. Beyond a gate, the route climbs through Castlehead Wood and then descends, beside a fence

▲ Looking down Glenridding Beck towards Ullswater and Place Fell

on the right, to the **B5289**. Cross over, turn left along a path on the other side of the hedge and then turn right. Entering Cockshot Wood, bear left and then keep right. Emerging from the trees, turn right along the lakeside lane to reach the **Derwentwater** landing stages and boat house.

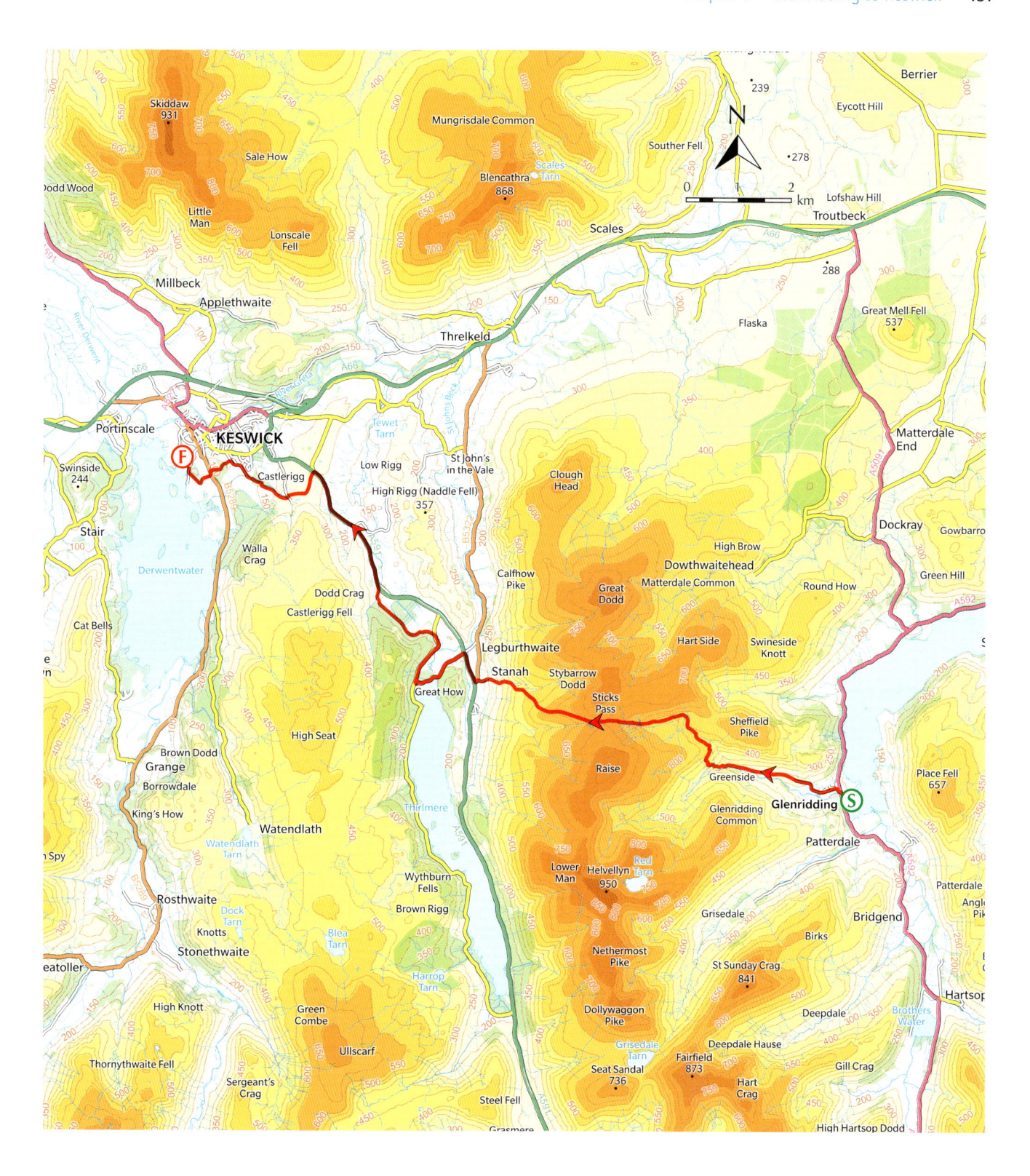

Chapter 9 – Glenridding to Keswick   131

CHAPTER 10
Keswick to Over Water
(Derwentwater, Bassenthwaite Lake, Over Water)

▲ Looking across the Derwentwater landing stages towards Skiddaw

Anyone who has ever spent any time in the Lake District in June knows about Cumbria's long, lingering twilights. For a couple of weeks either side of midsummer, the sun seems to spend hours lowering in the western sky, the shadows thrown out by the fells stretching languorously along the valley bottoms. Even when darkness does finally descend, a glow often remains in the far north-west – sometimes a blue streak, occasionally a hint of red along the horizon. As the night goes on, if the sky's clear and you've got a bit of altitude, you can watch as this glow shifts further north and north-east, a reminder that somewhere, not that many hundred miles away, daylight continues uninterrupted. But it was not to be for Joss on 25 June 1983. When he set off from the Blue Box in Keswick, it was dark. It would be good to be able to report that the fells were romantically silhouetted against the starry sky, watching over his final efforts on this long, challenging day, but they weren't; they were blanketed by cloud – invisible and oblivious. There was nothing external to stimulate him, to inspire or to reward; now, it was simply a case of getting his head down and getting on with it. This was to be the most gruelling section of the whole day; and

Derwentwater, Skiddaw and, just visible to the left, Bassenthwaite Lake ▶

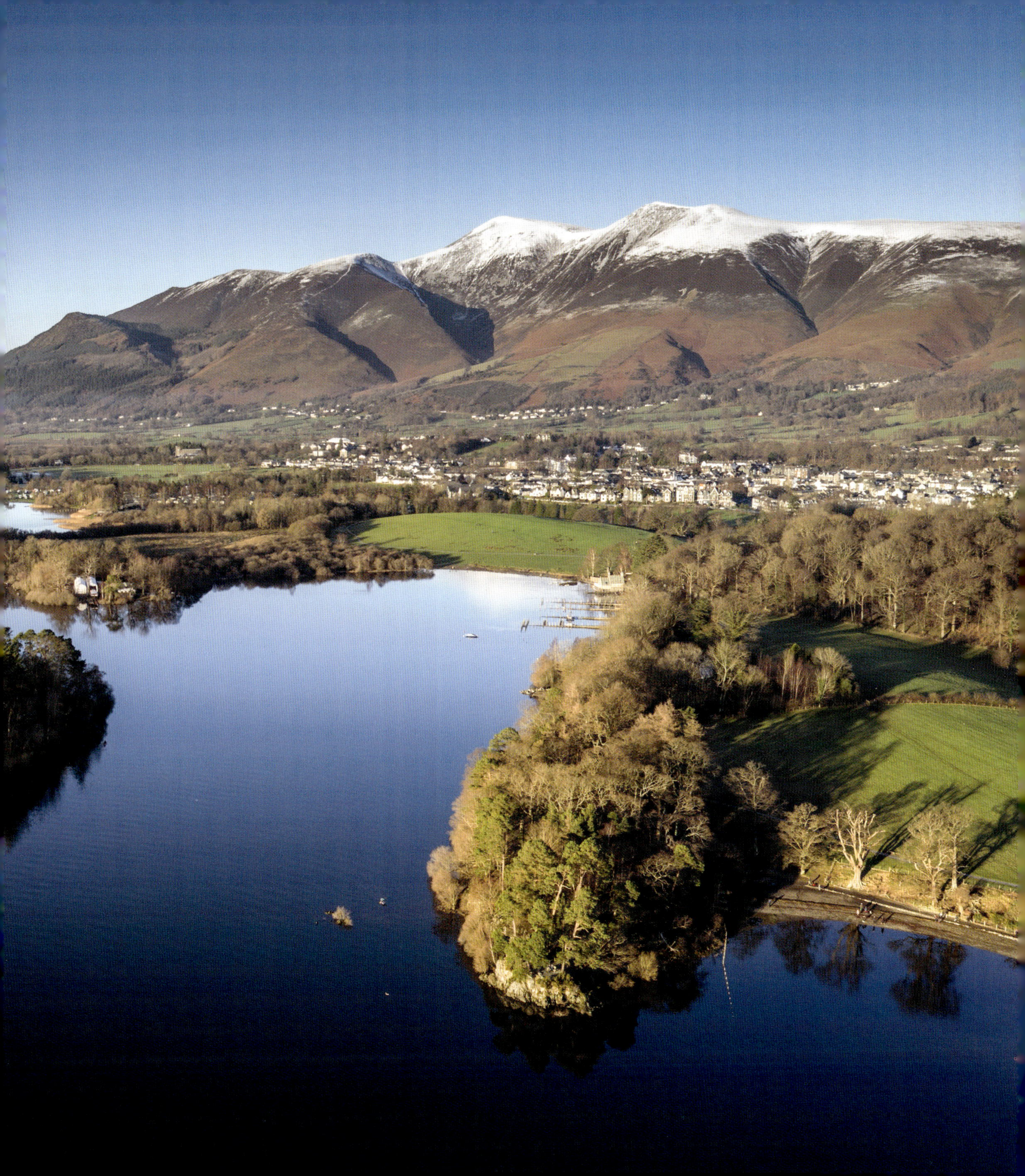

it was all to be completed on that most unforgiving of running surfaces – road.

He had a few runners accompanying him out of Keswick, hoping to bring a little cheer to these final miles. After the briefest of stops to acknowledge Derwentwater, the so-called 'Queen of the Lakes', they steered him through the town's streets. While drinkers loitered outside pubs, enjoying last orders, and holidaymakers headed back to their guesthouses after a night out, Joss dug in. When he and his entourage reached the unlit roads on the edge of town, they had a car in front of them, lighting the way, and another behind, protecting them from the traffic. He says it never felt unsafe. 'Back then, there wasn't so much traffic at night; there was only the odd car.'

The details of exactly where he left the road and reached the edge of Bassenthwaite Lake have been lost in the mists of time.

> While drinkers loitered outside pubs, enjoying last orders, Joss dug in

There aren't many places where the public can legitimately access the eastern shore, but, when your name is Joss Naylor and you're a local legend, doors (and sometimes farm gates) open for you. In his account of the day published in the January 1984 edition of *The Fell Runner*, Alex Smith wrote: 'The last tricky section was the approach to Bassenthwaite Lake where a local farmer let us stumble blindly through his field to the lake shore, willingly joining into the spirit of the occasion by providing a large torch and a good deal of cheerful banter.'

Today, one of the best places to reach the shore is from Dodd Wood, and it's there that the team head in 2020 to get photos (in daylight, of course) of Joss touching the water. From the conifer forests that cloak the western base of the Skiddaw massif, a path leads down past the elegant mansion of Mirehouse to St Bega's Church. Joss agrees it's a magical spot – a place where history and

▲ Ullock Pike provides the dramatic fell backdrop to St Bega's Church

landscape intertwine to bewitch even the most cynical. The tiny church itself, sitting just back from the edge of the lake, was built more than 100 years before the Norman conquest of England, on the site of an even earlier chapel. It's dedicated to an Irish princess who is said to have fled her homeland to escape an unwanted arranged marriage. Associated with several miracles, she lived a life of pious solitude on the Cumbrian coast and then in Northumbria. After Mirehouse was built in the 17th century and began receiving guests, the great and the good of British cultural life visited the religious site, among them the poets William Wordsworth and Alfred, Lord Tennyson, and the historian Thomas Carlyle.

Covering more than 1280 acres (520 hectares), Bassenthwaite Lake is the fourth largest lake in the National Park. (And, as every

> 'A local farmer let us stumble blindly through his field to the lake shore'

fond collector of useless facts will tell you, the only one to feature the word 'lake' in its name.) It is linked to its slightly larger neighbour, Derwentwater, by the River Derwent, meaning that its catchment is huge. The rain that falls on Sprinkling Tarn, situated at the northern end of the Scafell chain and famous for being the wettest place in the country, ends up here before flowing through Cockermouth and entering the Irish Sea at Workington. The theory is that, once upon a time, Derwentwater and Bassenthwaite Lake were probably one massive body of water.

Beyond Bass Lake, as it's known locally, Joss had just one more body of water on his list of 27. So, all downhill from here then? Unfortunately not. 'It's all up and down to Over Water,' Joss remembers. Assuming he touched the lake close to the Calvert Trust's outdoor activities centre at Little Crosthwaite, the next five miles

◀ A summer's day beside Derwentwater

Derwentwater and the surrounding fells seen from Dodd ▶▶

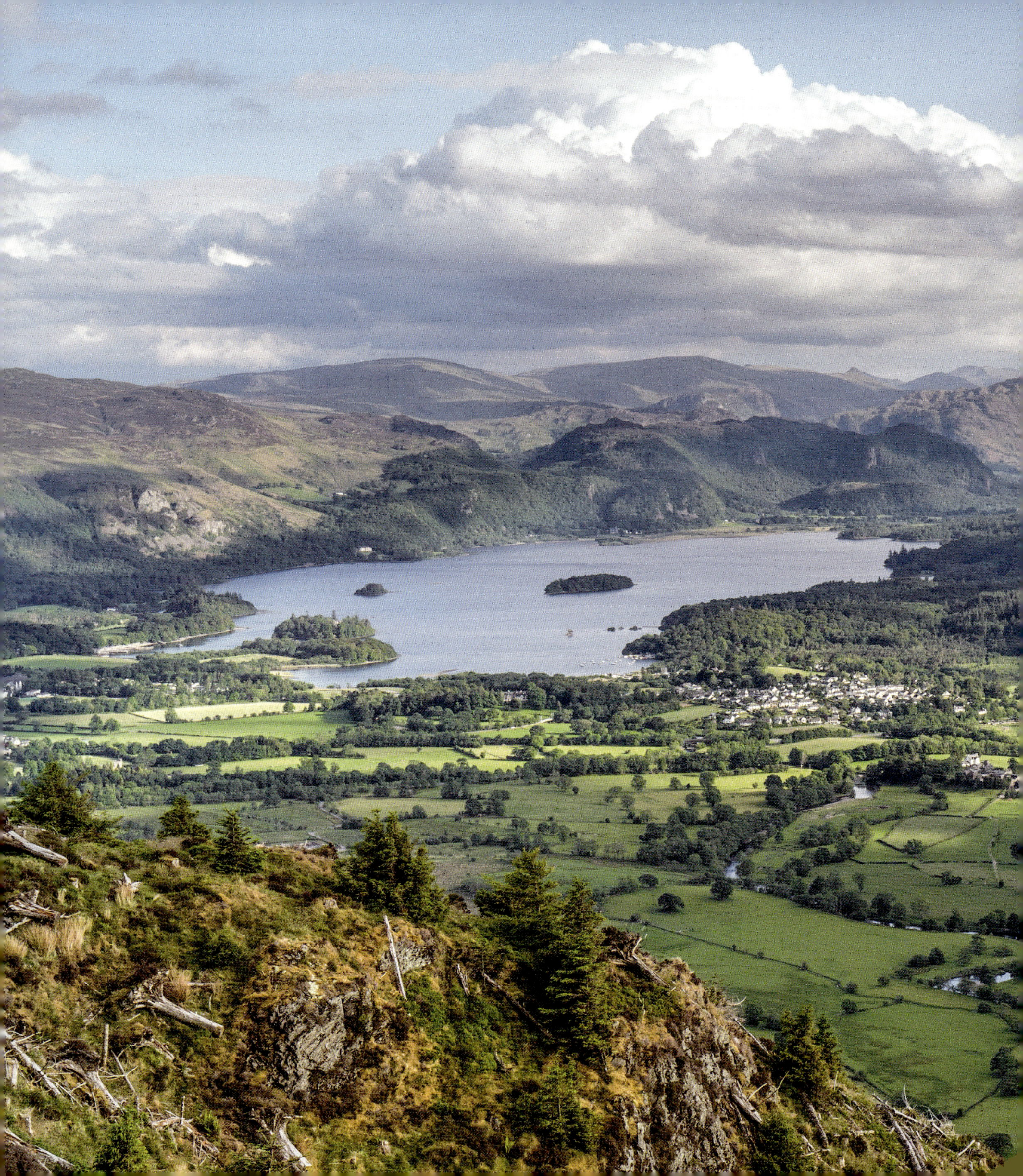

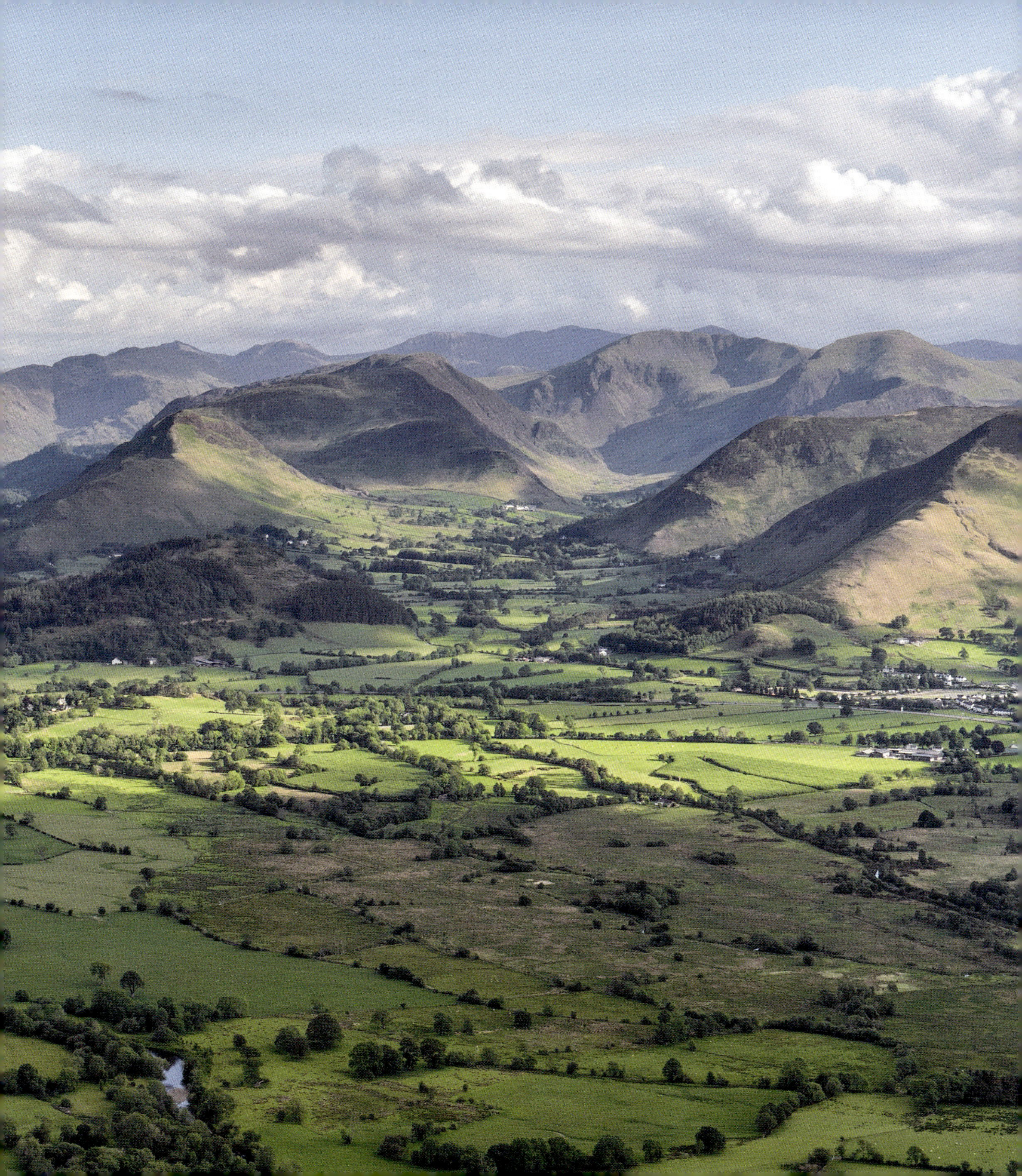

▲ Bassenthwaite Lake and (left) Skiddaw

to Over Water involved about 788ft (240m) of ascent and 481ft (147m) of descent – not much at all if you're just out for a gentle day's walk, but an excruciating total if you've already clocked up 100 miles on the fells. To make matters worse, the Orthwaite road had been resurfaced a few days earlier, and chippings had piled up along its edges. 'That was punishing – running on those stones. Three-quarter-inch chippings they were. I had to dig in. Not as bad as when I did the Coast to Coast though.'

Distracted by his memories again, Joss casts his mind back to the long, hot summer of 1976 when he completed a charity run from Ravenscar on the North Sea coast to St Bees in Cumbria – a total of 149 miles (240km) – in 40 hours. 'It was that bloody hot, the tarmac was running on the road. It burnt me feet badly and I had to walk from Tebay to St Bees Head, it was that painful. They were burning right through the night and I could hardly walk the next day.'

The stretch of road from Keswick to Over Water was the section that had nearly defeated Alan Heaton on his record-breaking run the previous summer. He'd never liked road running and, after a painful descent from Sticks Pass, ended up walking all the way from Thirlmere dam to Over Water. That wasn't an option for Joss though. 'It's no good – anybody who starts walking on that road, they don't run again if they've got all those miles in their legs,' he says. 'You've got to keep going.'

'Were you ever in any doubt that you'd manage it?' I ask him.

Chapter 10 – Keswick to Over Water 139

▲ The wooded shores of Bassenthwaite Lake

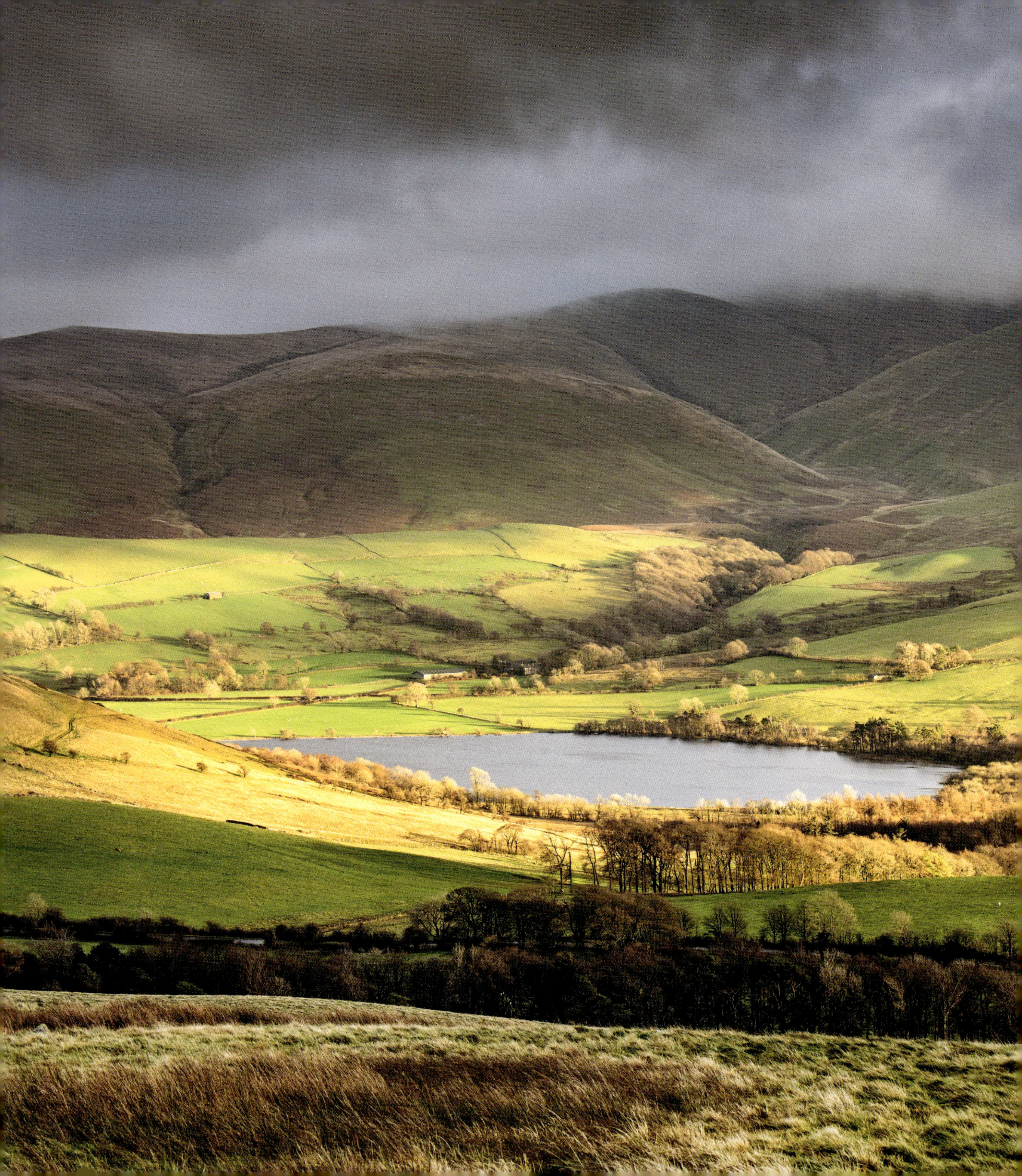

Chapter 10 – Keswick to Over Water   141

'I had it in me mind that I was gonna run it all, and that it was gonna be done on that schedule. It's mind over matter really.' Joss's steely determination is well documented, as is his unusually high pain threshold. Since he was a child, he has been plagued by back problems – caused by damage to discs in his lower spine when he was nine years old. An operation to put it right provided temporary relief, but another injury set him back again. The resulting crouched running style became one of his trademarks. 'They could recognise me from miles off.' Later in life, he also had to have all the cartilage in his right knee removed, but, despite the acute discomfort, he's always resisted doctors' pleas for him to have a knee replacement. For most people, such constant pain, tolerated for decades, is almost unimaginable. Couple that with the agony that comes naturally from endurance running, from pushing your body – any body – to its absolute limit, and you're in the realms of the superhuman.

Supporters lit the way for him with torches providing an avenue of light across the fields

He says he experienced little pain on his LMW run. 'It didn't bother us a lot that day. The pain I have is like someone putting a knife in it, the leg won't stride out. When my sciatic nerve's really bad, it's like dragging that leg. That day, there was little pain in the legs. Everything was right.' He recalls other times though when the pain has been so bad that he's passed out during races. 'It was mostly bad cramp that put me out. It'd be so severe, you'd pass out, but when you came round, it'd be gone.' He puts the cramp down to sciatic pain, stretching all the way from his back to his toes. 'Then there was that day Steve [Wilson] was with us when I fell off a crag in the Ennerdale Race. He said I fell 15ft, but I landed in a bed of heather. He shouts down to me, "Are you all right?" I said, "Aye." I tried to get up but I flaked out, like. When I came round, I held on to the stone for a couple of minutes and then walked through till Scarth Gap. I had blood running down me legs but I'd just knocked a bit of skin off. When I reached Scarth Gap, I looked down Ennerdale valley and I thought, "Well, me legs are still working..."' So he carried on to the finish line.

Nearing the finish line on the LMW, he pushed on through the final minutes of Saturday – still running, but slower now. It'd been a long day and everyone was tired – from the support team and marshals who had been following him around the Lake District practically since dawn to the runners who had joined him along the way and were now preparing for the grand finale. 'There was one or two lads running with us at that time, but there was very few words

◀ Over Water, day's end

▲ The 27th and final body of water

spoken.' Not surprising really. The only noise was some laboured breathing and the sound of runners' fatigued feet on the merciless road. Would it ever end?

Dave Elliott, who had been there right at the start of the day and was still there at the end, remembers it being very dark and narrow on this final stretch of the road. 'A number of those involved on the day had turned out,' he says. 'This resulted in a great trail of vehicles essentially blocking the single-track road. Sensibly, most of those parked in their cars turned on their headlights to illuminate the road ahead for Joss.'

Finally, Saturday having passed into Sunday, our tall, lean runner broke away from the road and made his way across country again. More supporters lit the way for him, this time with torches providing an avenue of light across the fields as he approached the southern shore of Over Water. 'There were a lot of people around at the finish,' he says. 'Some of the apprentices brought their families, and most of

▲ Made it! Joss, in borrowed Workington Zebras Rugby Football Club sweatshirt, at Over Water (Photo credit: Dave Elliott)

the runners were there too. It was good to see them there. The lads from work had never seen owt like that before. They couldn't believe that anyone could set off and run for that length of time – they'd seen us at five o'clock in the morning, and I was still running past midnight. It got one or two of them into running for a bit.'

Willing hands held down a barbed-wire fence for Joss to negotiate, and, according to Alex Smith, he hopped over it 'with remarkable ease'. Alex himself got caught in the wire. 'Having freed myself and stumbled across the field in the darkness I caught up with him just in time to get tangled up in the next fence,' he wrote. 'This time I didn't catch him until he arrived at the lakeside.'

Joss wasn't aware of Alex's entanglement; he just pushed on. He wasn't aware either that Dave had also disappeared. With just minutes to go, the official time-keeper had patted his pockets and realised he didn't have the stopwatches on him. 'I'd got proper timing watches and they were synchronised at Loweswater. I'd then put them in individual cases in the car to keep them safe,' he says. 'I started down the last fields with Joss but had barely covered two paces when I realised that, in the heat of the moment, I'd left them behind. It could've been disaster for the whole thing! With a few expletives ringing in the air, I quickly hopped back over the fence, sprinted back up, and grabbed them from the car. Fortunately for me, after 105 miles, Joss was travelling slower than earlier in the day and I caught him up in good time to record the official time as he paddled into his final lake.'

It was 14 minutes and 25 seconds past midnight on Sunday 26 June 1983 when Joss finally crouched down to touch Over Water. With that gesture, he had completed a 105-mile (169km) route involving nearly 20,000ft (6098m) of ascent and descent in 19hr 14min 25sec. He'd beaten Alan Heaton's record by more than six hours, and he'd done it within six minutes of his estimate. This is a man who, despite the scepticism of some, knew exactly what he was capable of.

As his supporters joined in a chorus of 'three cheers for Joss', he turned to Dave and asked what his time was. On hearing, he said: 'Well Dave, it's gonna tek a bloody good man on a bloody good day to beat that.' And he was right – as of July 2021, no man or woman has come anywhere near.

Did he celebrate? Was there champagne? Guinness, maybe? (One of Joss's favourite tipples.) No, he sat on the keel of an upturned rowing boat and gave a short speech of thanks – his thoughts quickly turning away from the accomplishment itself and towards all those people who had supported him.

'How did you feel though, Joss, knowing what you'd just achieved?' I ask him 37 years later.

His reply comes in his typically understated manner...'All right, aye.'

CHARITY EFFORTS

Mayfield School in Whitehaven and the Fourth Workington (St Michael's) Scouts were the two charities to benefit from Joss's 1983 run. The former, attended by children and young people with special educational needs, received a cash boost as a result of the run as well as a donation of computers from British Nuclear Fuels Ltd, Joss's employer at Sellafield. Joss had become involved with Mayfield through his friend and fellow Cumberland Fell Runners member, Tommy Orr, whose wife Audrey worked at the school.

As someone who had benefitted immensely from being in the Scouts, Dave Elliott saw his own involvement as a chance to help the Workington troop raise money to build a new headquarters. People bought tickets, guessing what Joss's final time would be. 'Some were ridiculous, expecting him to finish in five or six hours or a couple of days, but most, I was surprised, were fairly close, and six were within a minute or two,' says Dave. 'We sold about 3000 tickets and made a couple of thousand pounds from that. I remember sitting in my front room, sorting through all of them the day after the run, looking for the correct time. It took ages!'

Two of the main corporate sponsors were the West Cumbria Building Society and the local car dealer Graham & Bowness, both of which had provided T-shirts with their branding on them. Dave remembers the latter getting 'a little miffed' after Border TV news featured a pre-run interview with Joss in which he'd been wearing an old tracksuit top rather than their nice new T-shirt. 'I guess he wasn't really savvy to the sponsorship world at the time,' he says, laughing.

Joss ran the LMW for charity for a second time – in 1989. On this occasion, it was for leukaemia research, after a friend's daughter developed the illness. Instead of completing it in a day though, Joss and fellow runners (including Pete Todhunter, Geoff Clucas, Tony Jewell and David Donald) ran the 105 miles over several days, breaking it up with evening fundraising events in local hotels en route. While they did that, members of the West Cumbria Canoe Club did their bit by paddling the length of each of the lakes, meres and waters.

STAGE 10

Start	Derwentwater landing stages, Keswick (NY 264 227)
Finish	Parking area near Over Water's north-east shore (NY 255 353)
Distance	12 miles (19.3km)
Ascent	1410ft (430m)

Approximate walking time   5hr 30min–6hr 30min

▶ From the Derwentwater landing stages, head north along Lake Road. At Café Hope, as the walkway swings right to pass under the B5289, keep left along The Heads. Bear right when the road splits and then left along the B5289. Follow this round a sharp bend to the right and then go left at the mini roundabout.

▶ Turn left immediately after crossing the **River Greta** and then, in a few more metres, take the path on the right. Turn left along a surfaced lane, cross the suspension bridge over the **River Derwent** and immediately go through the gate on the right. Head downstream beside the river. After two gates, bear right when the path splits – to climb the embankment. Cross the road and take the path through the hedges opposite.

▶ Follow the river downstream. About 410 metres after passing under the **A66** road bridge, swing away from the river – aiming for the sheds of **How Farm**. Turn right along the concrete farm track and through a gate. At the far end of the first field, head left – through a pair of gates. A grassed-over track heads north through the middle of this field and then swings north-west part way through the next one. After a gate, veer roughly north again, later rejoining the **River Derwent** on its downstream journey.

▶ Cross at High Stock Bridge and follow the track to the **A591**. Turn left and take the next road on the right. After just 45 metres, turn sharp left along a forest road rising through **Dodd Wood**. At the second bend to the right, head west-north-west along a narrower trail. When this drops to a wider path, turn right. This later broadens to a forest road. Turn right at the next junction. Just after the osprey viewing platform, bear left at a fork and then go straight across at the next junction.

▶ The path drops to the **Dodd Wood** toilets and café. Leave the car park via the main vehicle entrance, turn left along the **A591** and go through the gate on the far side of the cottage opposite. Join a surfaced lane through the **Mirehouse** grounds. Keep to the left of the buildings and then straight on, aiming for St Bega's Church, just 155 metres back from the shores of **Bassenthwaite Lake**.

▶ From the church, retrace your steps for 55 metres and bear left to cross Skill Beck. The path, later broadening to a track, leads to a minor road. Turn left along this. After 0.6 miles (1km), take the broad, gated track on the right. At a sharp bend to the right, keep straight on – along a less well-used route. Pass to the right of the buildings at **Mire Side**. Join an access lane coming in from the right and follow this to the road. Turn right.

▶ Go straight over at the crossroads. On the edge of **Bassenthwaite** village, turn right beside the village green. Take the next lane climbing right, known as Back Hill. At the top, ignore the first gate. After the next gate, turn left, climbing with the field boundary on your left. Without a path on the ground, head east-north-east through the next two large fields, aiming for Kestrel Lodge in the distance. Go through a small gate and cross a slight hollow to reach a fence corner. Head uphill with the fence on your left. Beyond the next gate, veer north-east. Go through a gate and head east-north-east, keeping to the right of **Kestrel Lodge**. At a fenced strip of woodland, turn left through the gate, heading downhill with the field boundary. Ford a small beck and continue in the same direction. On the woodland edge, go through the gate on the right and drop half-left to a gate (hidden from view behind a solitary tree). Follow the trail down to the left and cross the footbridge over Halls Beck. Bear right.

▶ Cross the road to join a trail climbing steeply through the trees. Turn right at the top. Just beyond a stile and gate, you reach a track. Turn right along this. Follow it through one gate. Immediately before the second gate, turn left and climb beside the fence. After a ladder stile, veer north-east, staying above the gorse thicket but losing height. As the descent steepens, aim for the bridge 90 metres north of **Little Tarn**. Cross this and then climb the stile on the left. (Beware the aggressive buzzards in this area.)

▶ Never straying far from the field boundary on the right, head uphill and through a gate in the top corner. Continue with the fence on your right. In the field corner, turn right – through the gate – and aim for the creamy-coloured cottage at **Orthwaite**. Cross the stile in the wall and turn left along the road. Take the next road on the left. The **Over Water** parking area is on the right in 340 metres.

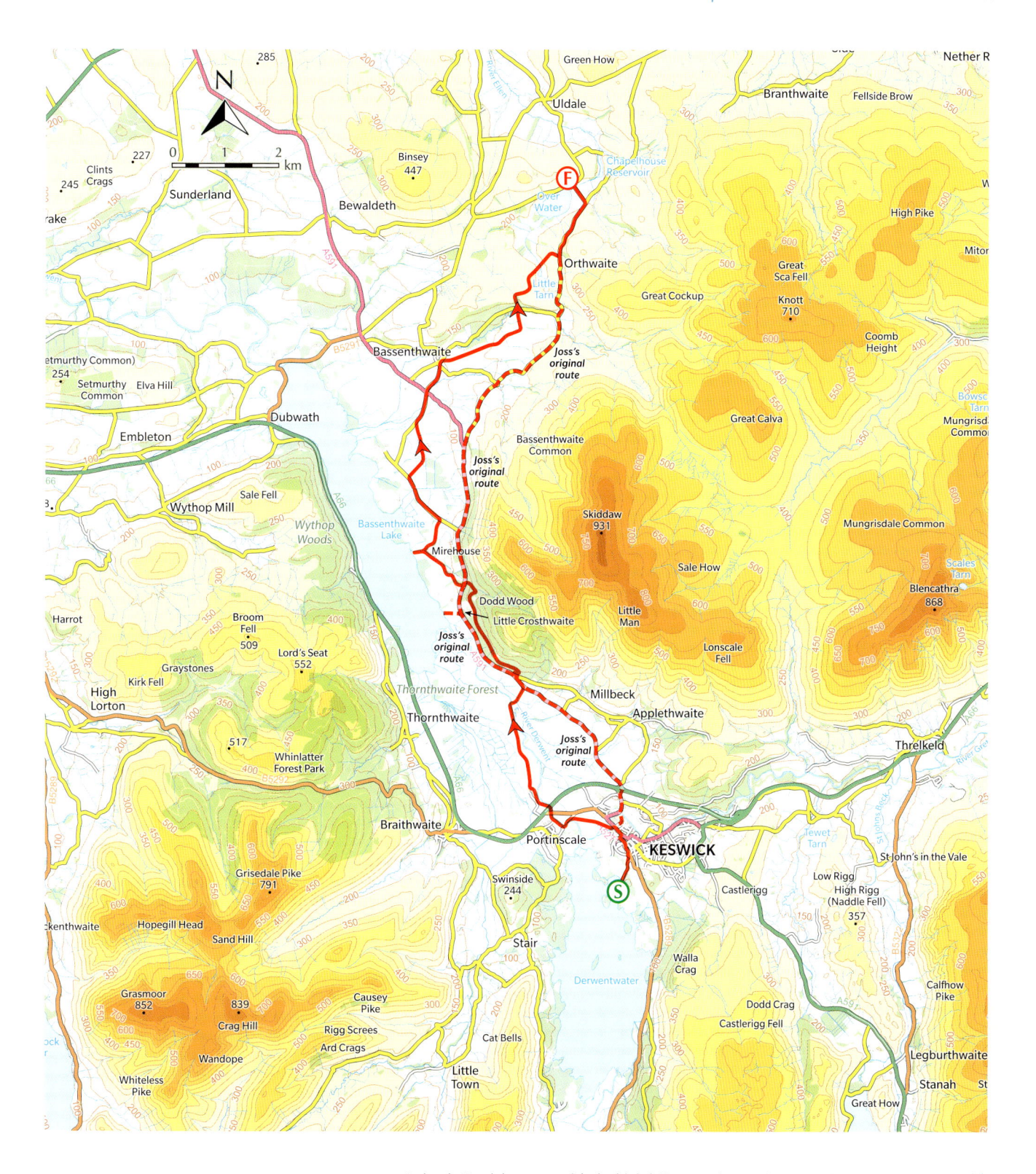

Chapter 10 – Keswick to Over Water   145

A classic Wasdale scene, with the high fells ranged around the top of the lake (Chapter 2) ▶▶

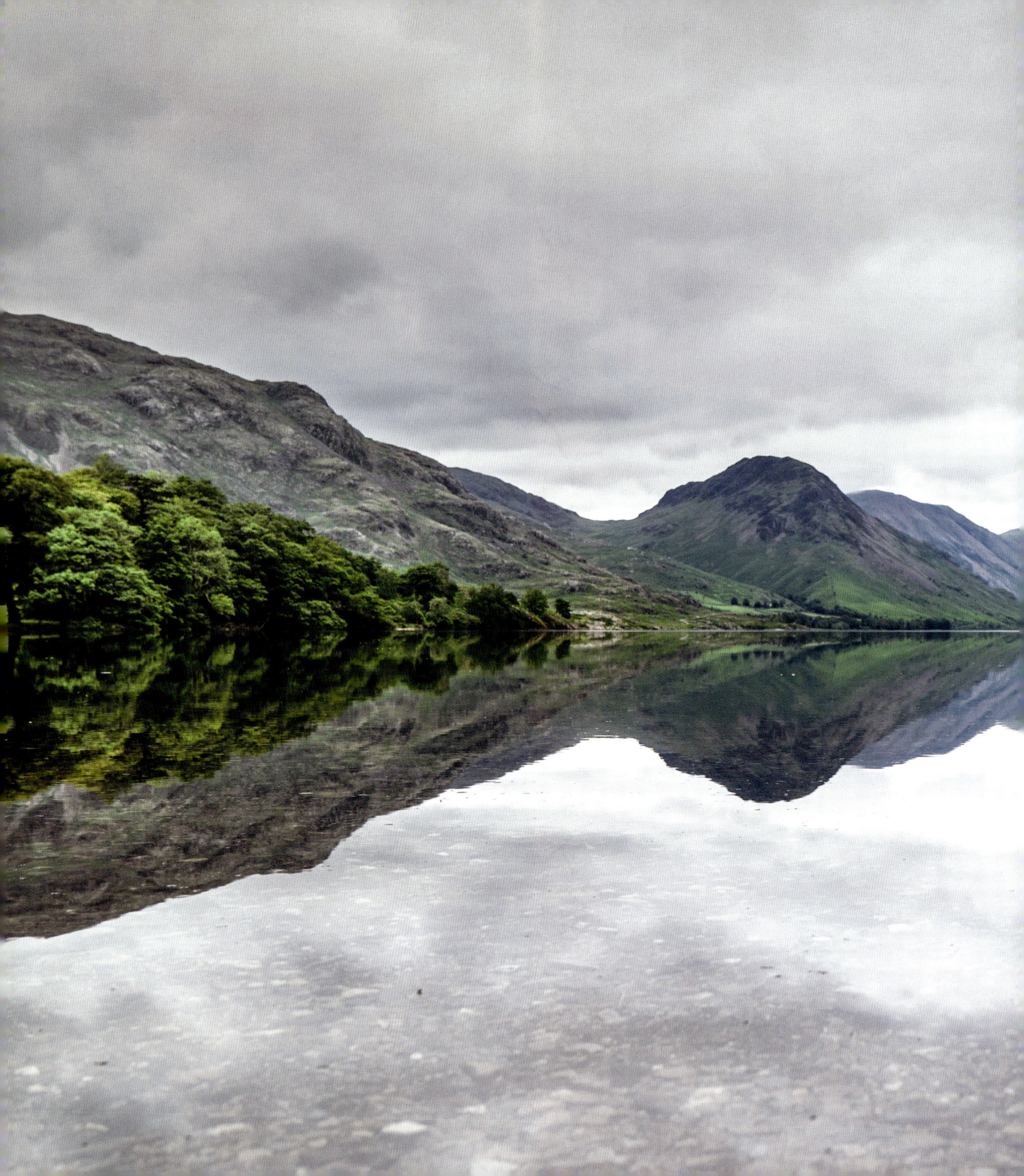

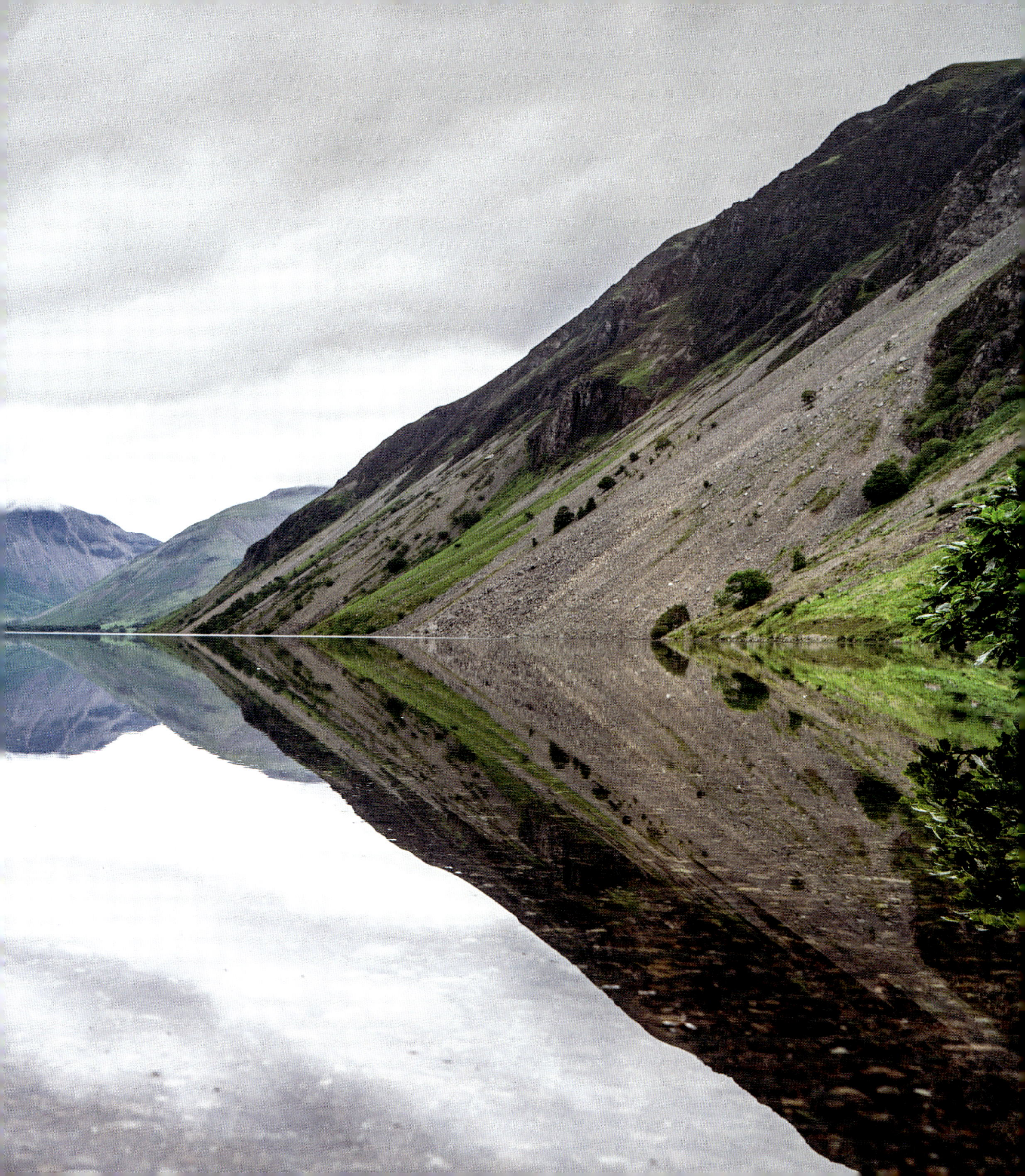

APPENDIX A
Marshals and split times for Joss's 1983 LMW

STAGE	STAGE NAME	MARSHALS	ESTIMATED TIME OF ARRIVAL	ACTUAL TIME
1	Loweswater	Support car	05.00	05.00
2	Crummock Water	Peter Blacklock, Alan Fisher	05.15	05.12
3	Buttermere	Ian Richardson	05.42	05.37
4	Ennerdale Water	Peter Carey, David Bailey	07.00	06.31
5	Wastwater	Joanne Cusick, Ian Cowan	08.30	07.58
6	Devoke Water	Alan Jackman	09.40	09.11
7	Goat's Water	John Stainton, Mark Carruthers	11.30	10.45
8	Low Water	Tom Bell, Neil McCracken	11.50	11.11
9	Levers Water	Mike Askew, George Nicholson	12.20	11.20
10	Coniston Water	Alastair Young, Graham Bell	12.30	11.43
11	Esthwaite Water	Rosemary Blenkinsop, Nicola Davies	13.20	12.27
12	Elter Water	Linda Spencer, Diane Brough	14.20	13.10
13	Grasmere	Andrew Hoodless, John Sumner	14.40	13.25
14	Rydal Water	Andrew Matterson	14.55	13.36
15	Windermere	Sean Silverwood	15.20	13.55
16	Skeggles Water	Peter Kerr, Andrew Simpson	17.10	16.03
17	Kentmere Reservoir	Andrew Sandelands, Philip Atherton	18.10	16.53
18	Small Water	Scouts	18.48	17.29
19	Blea Water	David Bailey, Ian Willey	18.58	17.38
20	Haweswater	Paul McDowell	19.20	17.56
21	Hayeswater	Scouts	20.10	19.06
22	Brothers Water	Ian Woodburn, Michael Quinn	20.30	19.29
23	Ullswater	Scouts	20.55	20.03
24	Thirlmere	Nigel Alderson, Gareth Hughes	22.15	21.35
25	Derwentwater	Mark Chapman	23.00	22.30
26	Bassenthwaite Lake	Support car	23.35	23.16
27	Over Water	Support car	00.20	00.14

APPENDIX B
The 27 lakes, meres and waters

(All figures are approximate)

NAME	SURFACE AREA	MAX DEPTH	ALTITUDE
Loweswater	0.23 square miles (0.6km^2)	52ft (16m)	397ft (121m)
Crummock Water	1 square mile (2.5km^2)	140ft (44m)	320ft (98m)
Buttermere	0.36 square miles (0.9km^2)	95ft (29m)	335ft (102m)
Ennerdale Water	1.2 square miles (3km^2)	138ft (42m)	375ft (114m)
Wastwater	1.1 square miles (2.9km^2)	249ft (76m)	200ft (61m)
Devoke Water	0.13 square miles (0.3km^2)	46ft (14m)	768ft (234m)
Goat's Water	0.01 square miles (0.03km^2)	43ft (13m)	1645ft (502m)
Low Water	0.01 square miles (0.02km^2)	46ft (14m)	1786ft (544m)
Levers Water	0.06 square miles (0.16km^2)	125ft (38m)	1350ft (415m)
Coniston Water	1.9 square miles (4.9km^2)	184ft (56m)	141ft (43m)
Esthwaite Water	0.39 square miles (1km^2)	51ft (16m)	216ft (66m)
Elter Water	0.06 square miles (0.16km^2)	23ft (7m)	187ft (57m)
Grasmere	0.23 square miles (0.6km^2)	72ft (22m)	207ft (63m)
Rydal Water	0.12 square miles (0.3km^2)	59ft (18m)	177ft (54m)
Windermere	5.7 square miles (14.8km^2)	210ft (64m)	128ft (39m)
Skeggles Water	0.02 square miles (0.05km^2)	10ft (3m)	1017ft (310m)
Kentmere Reservoir	0.06 square miles (0.16km^2)	Unknown	974ft (297m)
Small Water	0.02 square miles (0.04km^2)	53ft (16m)	1499ft (457m)
Blea Water	0.07 square miles (0.17km^2)	207ft (63m)	1601ft (488m)
Haweswater	1.51 square miles (3.9km^2)	187ft (57m)	787ft (240m)
Hayeswater	0.06 square miles (0.16km^2)	Unknown	1394ft (425m)
Brothers Water	0.01 square miles (0.02km^2)	49ft (15m)	515ft (157m)
Ullswater	3.44 square miles (8.9km^2)	207ft (63m)	476ft (145m)
Thirlmere	1.27 square miles (3.3km^2)	151ft (46m)	584ft (178m)
Derwentwater	2.09 square miles (5.4km^2)	72ft (22m)	249ft (76m)
Bassenthwaite Lake	2.05 square miles (5.3km^2)	62ft (19m)	226ft (69m)
Over Water	0.08 square miles (0.21km^2)	59ft (18m)	627ft (191m)

APPENDIX C
Glossary of dialect terms and topographical features

beck	stream, brook	*neebody*	nobody
bield	shelter (noun)	*nowt*	nothing
dale	valley	*owt*	anything
fell	hill, mountain	*rigg*	ridge
force	waterfall	*skop*	throw (verb)
gill	ravine, usually with a stream running through it	*summat*	something
hause	top of a pass, col	*tarn*	small mountain lake
la'al	little	*till*	to
lonning	lane, track	*tek*	take (verb)
mebbe	maybe	*tekken*	taken
mere	lake	*thwaite*	area cleared for farming
missel	myself	*us*	sometimes used instead of 'me'
moss	flat area, usually boggy	*yow*	ewe

APPENDIX D
Route summary table

These figures relate to the recommended route described at the end of each chapter, not the route Joss ran in 1983.

STAGE	START	FINISH	DISTANCE	ASCENT	WALKING TIME
1	Loweswater	Ennerdale	9.1 miles (14.7km)	2710ft (826m)	5hr–5hr 30min
2	Ennerdale	Eskdale Green	12.2 miles (19.6km)	3160ft (963m)	6hr 30min–7hr 30min
3	Eskdale Green	Dunnerdale	9 miles (14.5km)	1670ft (509m)	4hr 30min–5hr
4	Dunnerdale	Coniston	9.9 miles (15.9km)	3590ft (1095m)	6–7hr
5	Coniston	Skelwith Bridge	9.2 miles (14.8km)	1070ft (326m)	4hr–4hr 30min
6	Skelwith Bridge	Troutbeck	9.4 miles (15.1km)	1700ft (518m)	4hr 30min–5hr
7	Troutbeck	Haweswater	13.9 miles (22.4km)	3450ft (1052m)	7–8hr
8	Haweswater	Glenridding	9.4 miles (15.1km)	2470ft (753m)	5hr–5hr 30min
9	Glenridding	Keswick	11.9 miles (19.2km)	2500ft (762m)	6–7hr
10	Keswick	Over Water	12 miles (19.3km)	1410ft (430m)	5hr 30min–6hr 30min
		Totals	106 miles (170.6km)	23,730ft (7234m)	54–62hr approx

APPENDIX E
Some of Joss's challenge runs

Ramblers' Association's Lake District Four 3000ft Peaks Marathon Walk
(June 1970)
Distance: 45 miles (72km)
Time: 8hr 24min

24-Hour Fell Record
Joss broke this record on three separate occasions, with his 1975 record standing until 1988
June 1971 – 61 peaks in 23hr 37min, start/finish Wasdale
June 1972 – 63 peaks in 23hr 35min, start/finish Wasdale
June 1975 – 72 peaks in 23hr 11min, start/finish Keswick

National Three Peaks Challenge
(July 1971)
Ben Nevis, Scafell Pike and Snowdon, with Frank Davies driving – 11hr 54min

Welsh 1000m Peaks
(June 1972)
Distance: 25 miles (40km)
Time: 3hr 37min

The Fourteen Peaks
(June 1973)
The 3000ft peaks of Wales
Distance: 22 miles (35km)
Time: 4hr 46min

Pennine Way
(June 1974)
Distance: 271 miles (436km)
Time: 3 days 4hr 35min

Coast to Coast
(June 1976)
Distance: 149 miles (240km) from Ravenscar to St Bees
Time: 40hr

The 27 Lakes, Meres and Waters
(June 1983)
Distance: 105 miles (169km)
Time: 19hr 14min 25sec

The Wainwrights
(June 1986)
All 214 Lakeland tops listed in Wainwright's seven 'Pictorial Guides'
Approximate distance: 391 miles (629km)
Time: 7 days 1hr 25min
Joss's record stood until 2014

60 Peaks at 60
(June 1996)
At the age of 60, Joss ran 60 Lakeland peaks in 36hr 50min
Approximate distance: 110 miles (177km)

70 Peaks at 70
(July 2006)
At the age of 70, Joss ran 70 Lakeland peaks in less than 21hr
Approximate distance: 50 miles (80km)

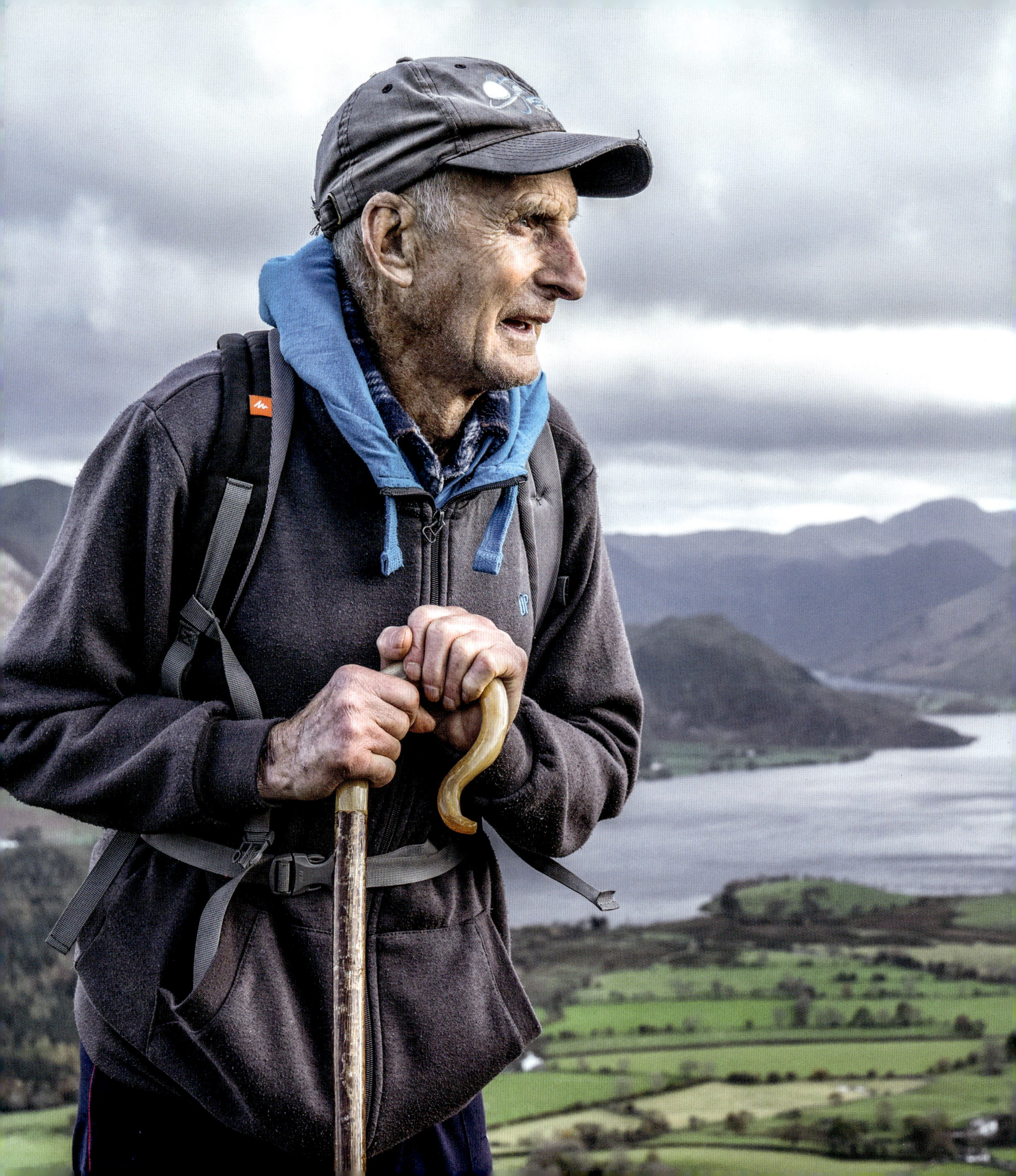

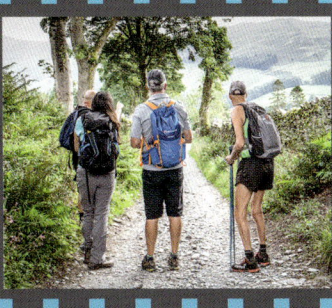

▲ Joss, Pete Todhunter and Vivienne Crow share a joke

▲ Joss with Pete, left, and Dave in the woods above Buttermere

▲ Joss with fell runner Sarah McCormack and her dogs

▲ The team stop to review the way ahead on Robin Lane

▲ Joss with fell runner Paul Tierney on High Street

▲ Joss with Vivienne at Hayeswater

▲ Joss and Pete enjoying lunch at Sticks Pass

▲ Resting with Pete beside Bassenthwaite Lake

◀ Joss on Low Fell, with Crummock Water behind (Chapter 1)

NOTES

NOTES

Transforming Young Lives

BRATHAY

Inspiring • Supporting
Sharing • Achieving

it all adds up to

Wellbeing

www.justgiving.com/brathay

- 🐦 @Brathay
- 📘 BrathayTrust
- 📷 brathaytrust
- in company/brathay

DOWNLOAD THE ROUTES IN GPX FORMAT

All the routes in this book are available for download from:

www.cicerone.co.uk/1087/GPX

as standard format GPX files. You should be able to load them into most online GPX systems and mobile devices, whether GPS or smartphone. You may need to convert the file into your preferred format using a conversion programme such as gpsvisualizer.com or one of the many other such websites and programmes.

When you follow this link, you will be asked for your email address and where you purchased the book, and have the option to subscribe to the Cicerone e-newsletter.

CICERONE

www.cicerone.co.uk

LISTING OF CICERONE GUIDES

BRITISH ISLES CHALLENGES, COLLECTIONS AND ACTIVITIES
Cycling Land's End to John o' Groats
The Big Rounds
The Book of the Bivvy
The Book of the Bothy
The C2C Cycle Route
The Mountains of England and Wales:
    Vol 1 Wales
    Vol 2 England
The National Trails
Walking The End to End Trail

SCOTLAND
Backpacker's Britain: Northern Scotland
Ben Nevis and Glen Coe
Cycle Touring in Northern Scotland
Cycling in the Hebrides
Great Mountain Days in Scotland
Mountain Biking in Southern and Central Scotland
Mountain Biking in West and North West Scotland
Not the West Highland Way
Scotland
Scotland's Best Small Mountains
Scotland's Mountain Ridges
Skye's Cuillin Ridge Traverse
The Ayrshire and Arran Coastal Paths
The Borders Abbeys Way
The Great Glen Way
The Great Glen Way Map Booklet
The Hebridean Way
The Hebrides
The Isle of Mull
The Isle of Skye
The Skye Trail
The Southern Upland Way
The Speyside Way
The Speyside Way Map Booklet
The West Highland Way
The West Highland Way Map Booklet
Walking Ben Lawers, Rannoch and Atholl
Walking Highland Perthshire
Walking in the Cairngorms
Walking in the Pentland Hills
Walking in the Scottish Borders
Walking in the Southern Uplands
Walking in Torridon
Walking Loch Lomond and the Trossachs
Walking on Arran
Walking on Harris and Lewis
Walking on Jura, Islay and Colonsay
Walking on Rum and the Small Isles
Walking on the Orkney and Shetland Isles
Walking on Uist and Barra
Walking the Cape Wrath Trail
Walking the Corbetts
    Vol 1 South of the Great Glen
    Vol 2 North of the Great Glen
Walking the Galloway Hills

Walking the Munros
    Vol 1 – Southern, Central and Western Highlands
    Vol 2 – Northern Highlands and the Cairngorms
Winter Climbs Ben Nevis and Glen Coe
Winter Climbs in the Cairngorms

NORTHERN ENGLAND TRAILS
Hadrian's Wall Path
Hadrian's Wall Path Map Booklet
The Coast to Coast Walk
The Coast to Coast Map Booklet
The Dales Way
The Dales Way Map Booklet
The Pennine Way
The Pennine Way Map Booklet
Walking the Dales Way
Walking the Tour of the Lake District

NORTH EAST ENGLAND, YORKSHIRE DALES AND PENNINES
Cycling in the Yorkshire Dales
Great Mountain Days in the Pennines
Mountain Biking in the Yorkshire Dales
St Oswald's Way and St Cuthbert's Way
The Cleveland Way and the Yorkshire Wolds Way
The Cleveland Way Map Booklet
The North York Moors
The Reivers Way
The Teesdale Way
Trail and Fell Running in the Yorkshire Dales
Walking in County Durham
Walking in Northumberland
Walking in the North Pennines
Walking in the Yorkshire Dales: North and East
Walking in the Yorkshire Dales: South and West

NORTH WEST ENGLAND AND THE ISLE OF MAN
Cycling the Pennine Bridleway
Cycling the Reivers Route
Cycling the Way of the Roses
Hadrian's Cycleway
Isle of Man Coastal Path
The Lancashire Cycleway
The Lune Valley and Howgills
Walking in Cumbria's Eden Valley
Walking in Lancashire
Walking in the Forest of Bowland and Pendle
Walking on the Isle of Man
Walking on the West Pennine Moors
Walks in Silverdale and Arnside

LAKE DISTRICT
Cycling in the Lake District
Great Mountain Days in the Lake District
Joss Naylor's Lakes, Meres and Waters of the Lake District

Lake District Winter Climbs
Lake District: High Level and Fell Walks
Lake District: Low Level and Lake Walks
Mountain Biking in the Lake District
Outdoor Adventures with Children – Lake District
Scrambles in the Lake District – North
Scrambles in the Lake District – South
The Cumbria Way
Trail and Fell Running in the Lake District
Walking the Lake District Fells –
    Borrowdale
    Buttermere
    Coniston
    Keswick
    Langdale
    Mardale and the Far East
    Patterdale
    Wasdale

DERBYSHIRE, PEAK DISTRICT AND MIDLANDS
Cycling in the Peak District
Dark Peak Walks
Scrambles in the Dark Peak
Walking in Derbyshire
Walking in the Peak District – White Peak East
Walking in the Peak District – White Peak West

SOUTHERN ENGLAND
20 Classic Sportive Rides in South East England
20 Classic Sportive Rides in South West England
Cycling in the Cotswolds
Mountain Biking on the North Downs
Mountain Biking on the South Downs
Suffolk Coast and Heath Walks
The Cotswold Way
The Cotswold Way Map Booklet
The Great Stones Way
The Kennet and Avon Canal
The Lea Valley Walk
The North Downs Way
The North Downs Way Map Booklet
The Peddars Way and Norfolk Coast path
The Pilgrims' Way
The Ridgeway National Trail
The Ridgeway Map Booklet
The South Downs Way
The South Downs Way Map Booklet
The Thames Path
The Thames Path Map Booklet
The Two Moors Way
The Two Moors Way Map Booklet
Walking Hampshire's Test Way
Walking in Cornwall
Walking in Essex
Walking in Kent
Walking in London
Walking in Norfolk

Walking in the Chilterns
Walking in the Cotswolds
Walking in the Isles of Scilly
Walking in the New Forest
Walking in the North Wessex Downs
Walking on Dartmoor
Walking on Guernsey
Walking on Jersey
Walking on the Isle of Wight
Walking the Jurassic Coast
Walking the South West Coast Path
Walking the South West Coast Path Map Booklets:
    Vol 1: Minehead to St Ives
    Vol 2: St Ives to Plymouth
    Vol 3: Plymouth to Poole
Walks in the South Downs National Park

WALES AND WELSH BORDERS
Cycle Touring in Wales
Cycling Lon Las Cymru
Glyndwr's Way
Great Mountain Days in Snowdonia
Hillwalking in Shropshire
Hillwalking in Wales – Vols 1&2
Mountain Walking in Snowdonia
Offa's Dyke Path
Offa's Dyke Path Map Booklet
Ridges of Snowdonia
Scrambles in Snowdonia
Snowdonia: 30 Low-level and easy walks – North
Snowdonia: 30 Low-level and easy walks – South
The Cambrian Way
The Ceredigion and Snowdonia Coast Paths
The Pembrokeshire Coast Path
The Pembrokeshire Coast Path Map Booklet
The Severn Way
The Snowdonia Way
The Wales Coast Path
The Wye Valley Walk
Walking in Carmarthenshire
Walking in Pembrokeshire
Walking in the Forest of Dean
Walking in the Wye Valley
Walking on Gower
Walking on the Brecon Beacons
Walking the Shropshire Way

INTERNATIONAL CHALLENGES, COLLECTIONS AND ACTIVITIES
Canyoning in the Alps
Europe's High Points

AFRICA
Kilimanjaro
The High Atlas
Walking in the Drakensberg
Walks and Scrambles in the Moroccan Anti-Atlas

ALPS CROSS-BORDER ROUTES
100 Hut Walks in the Alps
Alpine Ski Mountaineering
　Vol 1 – Western Alps
　Vol 2 – Central and Eastern Alps
Chamonix to Zermatt
The Karnischer Hohenweg
The Tour of the Bernina
Tour of Monte Rosa
Tour of the Matterhorn
Trail Running – Chamonix and
　the Mont Blanc region
Trekking in the Alps
Trekking in the Silvretta and Ratikon Alps
Trekking Munich to Venice
Trekking the Tour of Mont Blanc
Walking in the Alps

PYRENEES AND FRANCE/SPAIN CROSS-BORDER ROUTES
Shorter Treks in the Pyrenees
The GR10 Trail
The GR11 Trail
The Pyrenean Haute Route
The Pyrenees
Walks and Climbs in the Pyrenees

AUSTRIA
Innsbruck Mountain Adventures
The Adlerweg
Trekking in Austria's Hohe Tauern
Trekking in the Stubai Alps
Trekking in the Zillertal Alps
Walking in Austria
Walking in the Salzkammergut:
　the Austrian Lake District

EASTERN EUROPE
The Danube Cycleway Vol 2
The High Tatras
The Mountains of Romania
Walking in Bulgaria's National Parks
Walking in Hungary

FRANCE, BELGIUM AND LUXEMBOURG
Chamonix Mountain Adventures
Cycle Touring in France
Cycling London to Paris
Cycling the Canal de la Garonne
Cycling the Canal du Midi
Mont Blanc Walks
Mountain Adventures in the Maurienne
Short Treks on Corsica
The GR20 Corsica
The GR5 Trail
The GR5 Trail – Benelux and Lorraine
The GR5 Trail – Vosges and Jura
The Grand Traverse of the Massif Central
The Loire Cycle Route
The Moselle Cycle Route
The River Rhone Cycle Route
The Way of St James – Le Puy to the Pyrenees
Tour of the Queyras
Trekking in the Vanoise
Trekking the Robert Louis Stevenson Trail
Vanoise Ski Touring
Via Ferratas of the French Alps
Walking in Provence – East
Walking in Provence – West
Walking in the Ardennes
Walking in the Auvergne
Walking in the Briançonnais
Walking in the Dordogne
Walking in the Haute Savoie: North
Walking in the Haute Savoie: South
Walking on Corsica

GERMANY
Hiking and Cycling in the Black Forest
The Danube Cycleway Vol 1
The Rhine Cycle Route
The Westweg
Walking in the Bavarian Alps

IRELAND
The Wild Atlantic Way and Western Ireland
Walking the Wicklow Way

ITALY
Italy's Sibillini National Park
Shorter Walks in the Dolomites
Ski Touring and Snowshoeing
　in the Dolomites
The Way of St Francis
Trekking in the Apennines
Trekking in the Dolomites
Trekking the Giants' Trail: Alta Via 1
　through the Italian Pennine Alps
Via Ferratas of the Italian Dolomites Vols 1&2
Walking and Trekking in the Gran Paradiso
Walking in Abruzzo
Walking in Italy's Cinque Terre
Walking in Italy's Stelvio National Park
Walking in Sicily
Walking in the Dolomites
Walking in Tuscany
Walking in Umbria
Walking Lake Como and Maggiore
Walking Lake Garda and Iseo
Walking on the Amalfi Coast
Walking the Via Francigena
　pilgrim route – Parts 2&3
Walks and Treks in the Maritime Alps

MEDITERRANEAN
The High Mountains of Crete
Trekking in Greece
Treks and Climbs in Wadi Rum, Jordan
Walking and Trekking in Zagori
Walking and Trekking on Corfu
Walking in Cyprus
Walking on Malta
Walking on the Greek Islands – the Cyclades

JAPAN, ASIA AND AUSTRALIA
Hiking and Trekking in the Japan
　Alps and Mount Fuji
Hiking the Overland Track
Japan's Kumano Kodo Pilgrimage
Trekking in Tajikistan

HIMALAYA
Annapurna
Everest: A Trekker's Guide
Trekking in Bhutan
Trekking in Ladakh
Trekking in the Himalaya

NORTH AMERICA
The John Muir Trail
The Pacific Crest Trail

SOUTH AMERICA
Aconcagua and the Southern Andes
Hiking and Biking Peru's Inca Trails
Torres del Paine

SCANDINAVIA, ICELAND AND GREENLAND
Hiking in Norway – South
Trekking in Greenland – The Arctic Circle Trail
Trekking the Kungsleden
Walking and Trekking in Iceland

SLOVENIA, CROATIA, SERBIA, MONTENEGRO AND ALBANIA
Mountain Biking in Slovenia
The Islands of Croatia
The Julian Alps of Slovenia
The Mountains of Montenegro
The Peaks of the Balkans Trail
The Slovene Mountain Trail
Walking in Slovenia: The Karavanke
Walks and Treks in Croatia

SPAIN & PORTUGAL
Camino de Santiago: Camino Frances
Coastal Walks in Andalucia
Cycle Touring in Spain
Cycling the Camino de Santiago
Mountain Walking in Mallorca
Mountain Walking in Southern Catalunya
Portugal's Rota Vicentina
Spain's Sendero Historico: The GR1
The Andalucian Coast to Coast Walk
The Camino del Norte and Camino Primitivo
The Camino Ingles and Ruta do Mar
The Camino Portugues
The Mountains of Nerja
The Mountains of Ronda and Grazalema
The Sierras of Extremadura
Trekking in Mallorca
Trekking in the Canary Islands
Trekking the GR7 in Andalucia
Walking and Trekking in the Sierra Nevada
Walking in Andalucia
Walking in Menorca
Walking in Portugal
Walking in the Algarve
Walking in the Cordillera Cantabrica
Walking on Gran Canaria
Walking on La Gomera and El Hierro
Walking on La Palma
Walking on Lanzarote and Fuerteventura
Walking on Madeira
Walking on Tenerife
Walking on the Azores
Walking on the Costa Blanca
Walking the Camino dos Faros

SWITZERLAND
Switzerland's Jura Crest Trail
The Swiss Alpine Pass Route
　– Via Alpina Route 1
The Swiss Alps
Tour of the Jungfrau Region
Walking in the Bernese Oberland
Walking in the Engadine – Switzerland
Walking in the Valais
Walking in Zermatt and Saas-Fee

TECHNIQUES
Fastpacking
Geocaching in the UK
Map and Compass
Outdoor Photography
Polar Exploration
The Mountain Hut Book

MINI GUIDES
Alpine Flowers
Navigation
Pocket First Aid and Wilderness Medicine
Snow

MOUNTAIN LITERATURE
8000 metres
A Walk in the Clouds
Abode of the Gods
Fifty Years of Adventure
The Pennine Way – the Path, the People,
　the Journey
Unjustifiable Risk?

For full information on all our guides, books and eBooks, visit our website: www.cicerone.co.uk

CICERONE

Trust Cicerone to guide your next adventure, wherever it may be around the world...

Discover guides for hiking, mountain walking, backpacking, trekking, trail running, cycling and mountain biking, ski touring, climbing and scrambling in Britain, Europe and worldwide.

Connect with Cicerone online and find inspiration.

- buy books and ebooks
- articles, advice and trip reports
- podcasts and live events
- GPX files and updates
- regular newsletter

cicerone.co.uk